THE STUDENT LOAN SWINDLE

Why It Happened – Who Is To Blame – How The Victims Can Be Saved

By Bill Zimmerman

This book is dedicated to the millions of young Americans whose lives have been severely diminished by the student loan swindle.

Table of Contents

Chapter 1: Why The Solution Requires Radical Action

If you accepted a federal loan to go to college or a private student loan from a bank, you were swindled. The student loan apparatus in the United States is packaged to look like nurturing support for college students. In fact it is a system designed to exploit them, to transfer from their families and their future earnings many billions of dollars that have become the undeserved profits of the banking industry.

If you still struggle to repay one of these deceptive loans, you are not alone. Millions of ex-students have also been left in a deep financial hole, a hole that not only limits their lives, financially and otherwise, but one that is also undermining the larger economy.

In 2010, the government took one half-step toward improving the federal loan system, but that change only affected new loans going forward. Since then, in spite of a few attempts that were mere window-dressing, no meaningful relief has been delivered to people like you, nor is any under serious consideration by any agency of government.

It is the purpose of this short book, first, to explain what went wrong – why the student loan crisis happened and who was responsible – and second, to help borrowers plan their escape from the financial hole in which they are trapped.

The tens of millions of federal student loans and all the private bank loans made so far were deeply flawed and grossly unfair. The federal government not only ignored this unfairness but actively promoted it, passing laws that gave the banking industry guaranteed profits and undue leverage over student borrowers. This will be documented at length. For now, it is important to realize, if you haven't already, that a great injustice has been perpetrated on American college students and their families.

Because of its magnitude, correcting this injustice will not be easy. Any meaningful solution will oblige both the government and the banks to relinquish billions of dollars of debt owed to them by student borrowers. That means each will use all the power at its disposal to block genuine reform. A radical out-of-the-box strategy is required, one that goes outside conventional structures of law and commerce.

Can such a struggle actually be won? Yes. There is a practical plan that would provide real financial relief for all victims of the student loan crisis. It will be outlined in detail in the closing chapters of this book. Understanding the need for such a plan, and executing it effectively, requires a thorough understanding of the student loan system, how it evolved, why it became exploitive, and who was responsible for perverting it. That will be provided in the coming chapters, but first here is a brief overview of the whole picture.

****

The federal government made a fundamental error when it first created the student loan program. It was an error that led to the financial exploitation of millions of students. The 1965 Higher Education Act signed by President Johnson was the first large-scale expansion of federal student loans. However, instead of the government providing money directly to students, the law allowed private banks to put up the cash with the government guaranteeing repayment.

That mistake violated the principals of a free-market economy by creating a risk-free business for the banking industry. It led the banks to commit massive interest rate and collection abuse (and eventually outright fraud), which will be described in the coming chapters. It also moved a massive amount of money from middle and working class families to the banking industry, and as a result, it became a significant cause of the widening wealth and income inequality that currently undermines our economy.

Another error made by the government came later and was even more egregious. Not merely a mistake, it was an act of official discrimination. Unlike all other legal borrowers, the federal government deprived students of the right to discharge their student loan debt through bankruptcy, even if circumstances beyond their control left them unable to repay it.

Given that a well-paying job is necessary to repay a student loan, and given our society's increasing inability to provide such jobs to recent college graduates, millions of Americans are now unable to make regular payments on their outstanding student loans. Many never will. Without access to bankruptcy, their debts will stay with them until they die, and will continually increase because of ongoing penalties and fees. There was no reason for government to repeal bankruptcy protection on student loans other than its desire to protect the profits of the banks.

In 2010, President Obama corrected the first error by removing the banks from the federal student loan program and ordering all subsequent federal loans to be made directly from the Treasury. Since these loans are too few and too small to satisfy all the students who will need them, private banks continue to make supplemental loans to students and their families at exorbitant interest rates.

President Obama also ordered a new repayment system for some post-2010 federal student loans. That system is a step in the right direction, but again it only applies to new loans made after 2010. Under this system, there is no fixed monthly payment due. Instead, the monthly repayment requirement is 10% of the debtor's discretionary income, the amount left after paying for basic necessities. No late fees or penalties are imposed even if income is too low to require any payment at all.

If qualifying borrowers make these payments when they can, regardless of the size of the payment made, and if they continue to do so for a period of twenty years, any unpaid balance is then automatically forgiven, thus removing the need for bankruptcy protection and protecting borrowers during periods of under-employment. This program will be described in detail, but keep in mind that it does not affect federal loans made before 2010 or any private bank loans.

Those who labor under pre-2010 federal debt and/or private bank loans have been left stranded. Neither government nor the banking industry has proposed any significant measures to bring them meaningful relief. Instead, a blizzard of confusing alternatives has been presented that are so complicated they require loan consultants and accountants to decipher. These proposals are a smokescreen designed to hide the deeper reforms needed.

Real reform would force the banking industry to relinquish billions in anticipated income, so despite ample evidence that these loans were unfair to students, that government bent the rules to help the banks, and that profits were realized far in excess of what might be expected under the usual rules of commerce, no relief can be realistically anticipated.

After President Obama used his executive authority in 2010 to change the federal loan system, Congress thwarted attempts at further reform. In their 2013 session, they spent the entire first half of the year in hot debate about one single aspect of the crisis: how to cap interest rates on future federal student loans. After six months, they failed to agree. Public outrage then forced passage of a limit too small to take seriously.

But, unfortunately, that extensive debate in Congress helped create the mistaken impression that problems resulting from the student loan crisis are being addressed. They aren't. All that sound and fury was about future loans. Interest rates on the pre-2010 federal loans and all the private bank loans remain excessive for students and highly profitable for banks. Many are locked in place by the original loan contracts, while the available opportunities to refinance are on terms favorable only to the banks.

The crisis caused by student loans is a societal disaster. More than 37 million Americans carry pre-2010 federal student debt, and unknown millions more are in debt to the private banks. Collectively, they owe $1.15 trillion. That amount is one and a half times the total credit card debt in the country. An unknown but large number of these unsecured loans will never be repaid. If too many go into default, it will throw another monkey wrench into the U.S. economy similar to the housing loan crisis in 2008.

Remarkably, this crisis is visible to everyone. Academic experts and government officials have publicly decried the impending disaster. The press has extensively covered the story. Yet so powerful are the Wall Street banks benefiting from student loans that no real solutions are even up for debate, either in government or the press. Student loan borrowers desperately struggling to keep up have been abandoned. Those already in default were left with increasing debt they will never be able to repay.

Excessive debt disqualifies student loan borrowers from other credit, especially if they are in default or their payments are delinquent. Without credit they cannot buy homes or cars, get business loans, or even rent apartments. They are less likely to marry and have children. Parents who assisted them, for example by co-signing bank loans, are forced into debt themselves and suffer similar economic constraints.

This is not just a problem for the borrowers. It affects everyone. In April 2013, commenting on the hardships faced by the borrowers, researchers at the Federal Reserve Bank of New York said that their "lowered expectations of future earnings and more limited access to credit may have broad implications for the ongoing recovery of the housing and vehicle markets, and of U.S. consumer spending more generally."

A plan to free the victims from this financial trap requires three elements. First, evidence must show that government structured federal student loans in a way that gave the banking industry permission to engage in astonishing acts of greed and misconduct. Without clear evidence of governmental malfeasance, the extraordinary measures required to correct the situation will not be possible.

Second, a fair solution must be developed, one that grants lenders the right to recover some of the money they lent while preventing borrowers from escaping responsibility for having spent the money they received, a result that would be grossly unfair to other borrowers who have already sacrificed mightily to pay what they could.

Third, there must be a strategy that gives the victims sufficient political power to *force* this solution on the government and the banks whether they like it or not. This strategy must overcome the relative weakness of the borrowers just as it limits the overwhelming strength of their opponents. Force is necessary because the government and the banks will vigorously oppose any settlement costing them so much money.

To satisfy the first requirement, the fifty-year history of student loans that follows will reveal that from the very beginning they were unfair and exploitive, that the government ignored its obligation to protect the borrowers, that laws were passed that gave an undeserved commercial advantage to lenders, that government unfairly profited itself and helped the banking industry gather many billions in undeserved earnings, and that politicians of both parties helped advance these injustices.

The second requirement, a fair settlement that would end the crisis and bring relief to the borrowers can be achieved with only two major reforms: lowering interest rates on all outstanding federal and private student loans to non-profit levels, and rescheduling payments on all such loans based on the borrower's income.

Non-profit loans mean that the borrower pays the same interest rate the lender pays to get the money lent. Banks borrow money from the Federal Reserve at what is called the discount rate. In 2013 and early 2014, that rate was 0.75%. As you will soon see, banks have already made enough profit on student loans to last them for generations. Just as we commonly require public utilities to offer lifeline rates to senior citizens in exchange for the right to maintain their monopolies, banks can now be required to provide non-profit interest rates to students in exchange for those profits and for the bailout and other support they regularly receive from government.

Rescheduling payment is the second reform. Like the new system for post-2010 federal loans, instead of fixed monthly payments, borrowers would be required to pay 10% of their discretionary income, whatever it is. If any outstanding balance remains after twenty years, it would be forgiven. Details will be provided later, but the virtue of this system is that it overcomes the lack of bankruptcy rights and allows under-employed borrowers to remain creditworthy and able to function economically.

Repayment based on income also allows the banks to recover as much of the money they lent as possible without ruining the borrower. In addition, it prevents borrowers from scamming the system by requiring them to pay a portion of whatever they earn. No one will escape consequences for having spent money they borrowed, and those borrowers who have already struggled to repay their loans will have nothing to resent. If this system is fair for some of the post-2010 federal loans, it should be fair for all student loans.

The third requirement, a strategic plan to force this solution on the government and the banking industry, may seem beyond our reach but as you will see it is not. To begin with, our opponents will argue that government lacks the authority to revise existing loan contracts, and they will use their lobbying muscle to block any legislation that tries to do so.

Since real reform will be seen as a political impossibility, no elected official will risk providing leadership.

But government does have the authority to intervene in the economy and implement these two reforms. Various ordinary and emergency powers and precedents are available. Similar authority was used to close banks during the Great Depression, to seize the entire steel industry in 1952, and to impose national wage and price controls in 1971. Understandably, government is reluctant to use these powers and rarely does so, and of course it would be foolhardy to think such action would be taken on behalf of politically powerless student loan borrowers. That's why *force* is necessary, and why a strategy of civil disobedience is required.

That strategy, the third element in the plan, may seem hopeless yet it is feasible. But *forcing* solutions in a democratic society sets a dangerous precedent. Only in cases in which there is no other way to correct a grave injustice should it even be considered. That is why a strategy involving force must be justified and supported, first by a thorough understanding of the history of the injustice, and second by a fair plan for its resolution.

A potentially successful strategy is available from our country's rich history of boycotts, strikes, occupations and sit-ins. Think for a moment about a typical rent strike. Tenants in a building petition a negligent landlord to make necessary repairs. They are ignored. They exhaust all reasonable options but to no avail. Finally, the tenants decide to stop paying rent until the repairs are made.

The landlord's bills pile up: utilities, property tax, mortgage payments, maintenance. There is no cash flow from rental income to cover these bills. If the landlord evicts all the tenants, it will take months to get through the courts and then more months to find new tenants. Complying with tenant demands is often the cheapest way out. In cases like this, the side that holds out the longest wins. If the tenants stay united, and are able to resist the various forms of intimidation available to the landlord, they usually prevail.

Entities that lend money, like banks and even the federal government, have a cash flow like landlords. Both have a steady income from the monthly repayment checks they receive, and because the bulk of a bank's assets are tied up in investments, while the government's are needed for ongoing obligations, both use their monthly income to meet part of their expenses.

If that monthly cash flow stops, they are in trouble. This vulnerability can be exploited, and the Internet and social media present a unique opportunity to do so on a massive scale. Imagine the impact if a large portion of the 37 million Americans with outstanding federal student debt and the millions more who owe money on private bank loans launched a payment strike.

It might work like this. An Internet website is built that allows borrowers to pledge to withhold all further loan repayments if and when five million others pledge to do so at the same time. The threat would be withdrawn if the interest rate on all student debts, federal and private, past, present and future, is reduced to the Federal Reserve's discount rate, and the repayment schedules for all such loans are made dependent on the borrower's income.

Five million participants is a huge goal, but with tens of millions holding outstanding student debt, and suffering various forms of abuse, it is doable. Problems are so widespread that six million borrowers are already in default. They no longer make payments, so they are unable to provide any leverage. But another twelve million are chronically late with their payments, a rich field from which to recruit, along with the many millions more who struggle to keep up.

Making such a pledge is not as risky as it seems. There is no legal or other jeopardy involved in making a pledge. It is only when payments are actually withheld that jeopardy begins. Many will make the pledge as a protest only, not yet ready to actually commit. This creates a powerful potential not present in a rent strike where the threshold act is to actually stop paying rent. In a payment strike like this, where only a pledge is required, numbers can build to a point where those who had intended only to protest can see the potential power inherent in their numbers and deepen their commitment.

When the number of pledges grows into the millions, and the motivation of those pledging is nurtured and preserved through frequent contact with the website, pressure on government to find a solution will increase dramatically. The news media will jump on the story given that it pits so many ordinary Americans against the federal government and the most powerful banks in the country, the same banks that many now blame for other flaws in our economy. Various interest groups unconnected with student loans will weigh in for or against the potential payment-strikers. That will heighten news coverage, aid in recruiting more borrowers, and add urgency to the search for a solution.

Do not underestimate the possibility that governmental resistance will collapse before the pledges have to be honored. If it doesn't, and payments are withheld, like the landlord unable to evict all of his tenants, the government and the banks cannot simultaneously or effectively take action against millions of striking borrowers. They would threaten to do so, and they would go after a few as examples. But if the payment-strikers stuck together and resisted intimidation, few would suffer any consequences and in the end all would be victorious.

There is a detailed description of how to use the Internet to organize a payment strike in the last chapter of this book. For now, keep in mind that no matter how powerless people may be, they possess a passive weapon as robust as any their opponents have: the power to refuse, to say no. If millions of payment-strikers can bring themselves to say no, tens of millions of fair-minded Americans will give them their sympathy and their support.

Instead of an isolated rent strike in a single building against a single landlord, the battle over the student loan crisis can put government in the middle between aroused public opinion on the one hand and the country's most powerful financial institutions on the other. That is a battle many would like to fight, because when government is stuck in the middle like that, their vulnerability allows for other gains to be made as well.

I see no feasible strategy for fixing the student loan crisis other than one based on civil disobedience. The lobbying power and legislative influence of the big banks and the degree to which Congress has become dependent upon their campaign contributions and lobbying money preclude, in my view, any reasonable compromise.

So, to justify the use of force through a strategy of civil disobedience, let's take a much closer look at the student loan crisis: why were these loans created in the first place, how did anti-student bias and banking greed corrupt the system, why did the cost of college tuition escalate so dramatically, how much money was made on the backs of the students, and what role did political ideology play in justifying this mess.

Chapter 2: Who Are the Victims of the Student Loan Crisis?

Most of the students who received bank loans or federal loans before 2010 believed they were getting a good deal, that a college degree would increase their earning power. They assumed a well-paying job awaited them after graduation, a job that would provide enough to live decently and pay down their debt. They did what they were supposed to do, but for many of them a job with the salary they had hoped for was nowhere to be found. They were left holding the bag – and all that was in it were thousands of dollars of debt and a stack of collection notices.

If you are one of those victims, you must first understand that your inability to repay your college loan is not your fault. There are millions of others in the same fix, which means that the fault for the overall mess is much more likely to be with the system that made the loans than with the individuals who did the borrowing. Take a good look at the overall student loan system and its history and you will understand.

Over the past thirty years, the cost of a college education went up much faster than any other element in the overall cost of living, including health care. College became unaffordable for working and middle class families. As a result, students needed ever-larger loans to cover their expenses. For a system like this to work, graduating students require the kind of jobs that are now rapidly disappearing.

Good jobs began to vanish before the 2008 recession, but when the recession hit, the bottom truly fell out of the jobs market. In 2012, Northeastern University's Center for Labor Market Studies estimated that slightly more than half of young college graduates either could not find jobs at all, were working in unpaid internships, or were employed flipping hamburgers or in other low-wage capacities. Most had severe loan repayment requirements they were unable to maintain.

Two lines on a graph illustrate the problem. The first shows the massive increase in the college population, from 8.5 million in 1970 to 21.1 million in 2010. The second displays the number of good entry-level jobs for college graduates, jobs that come with decent pay, benefits, and opportunities for advancement, a number that is difficult to measure but one that is now in relentless decline. For many years, the two lines went up in parallel. Now, the second drops farther and farther behind every year. This is the trap that is undermining the financial future of so many ex-students.

The crisis affecting them is much bigger and more important to the overall economy than many realize. The fact that 37 million Americans have outstanding pre-2010 federal student debt means that one in five American households are affected, not counting others with private bank debt. Another million debtors are added every year. In 2012, the average student debt was $26,600. And if you think the people involved are merely the poor and the marginal, guess again. A study of 2011 financial disclosure forms by OpenSecrets.org revealed that five U.S. Senators and 41 Members of Congress are among them.

Of the 37 million with pre-2010 federal loans, a staggering six million are already in default. "Default" means that no payments have been made for nine months. About twice that number are "delinquent," which means they have missed at least two payments. Thus, 18 million people, or about half of these pre-2010 borrowers, are either unable to pay at all or are undergoing real hardship to do so. In 2013, the Consumer Financial Protection Bureau also estimated that there are at least 850,000 private loans in default. This massive percentage of failed loans should make it crystal clear that the fault lies with the system and not with the individual borrowers.

The amount of money involved is also staggering. Roughly $1 trillion is owed on pre-2010 federal loans, while it is estimated that another $150 billion is owed to banks for private loans. To put that in perspective, in 2012 all the credit card debt in the country totaled $672 billion, only two-thirds of the combined student loan debt.

Several agencies, including the U.S. Treasury Department's Office of Financial Research, the Federal Reserve, the Financial Stability Oversight Council and the Consumer Financial Protection Bureau, have all warned that the vast amount due on outstanding student loans, some of which will never be repaid, is a threat to the stability of the entire American economy. Ben Bernanke, Federal Reserve chairman at the time, said, "To the extent that there's a lot of student debt held by people who are not working, it's obviously yet another drag on recovery." That's why the student loan crisis is so important, not just to struggling borrowers but to all Americans.

With so many millions owing so many billions, it's important to understand the mechanics. When loan payments are not made, the loans get bigger. Interest on the original principal (the amount borrowed) continues to accumulate even though payments have stopped. That accumulating interest is added to the current principal (the total amount still owed), which then triggers even higher monthly interest charges. Meanwhile, because a payment was missed, late fees and other penalties are assessed and also added to the principal. Because of these accumulating charges, the loan amount that many borrowers began with has doubled or even tripled: such being the wonders of compound interest.

The most crippling problem that affects ex-student borrowers in trouble is the absence of bankruptcy protection. Unlike other borrowers, they are legally prevented from discharging their debt through bankruptcy no matter how difficult their other burdens or how unlikely they will ever have the resources with which to repay it. Without this protection, troubled borrowers are permanently harnessed to their loans. No other borrowers have been deprived of this basic protection except those whose debts originate in criminal, illegal or negligent behavior. The result: these former students either repay their loans or live with their debt until they die.

If you have student debt you are unable to repay, your financial life will be limited. You will be unable to buy anything on credit. Loans for graduate or professional school will not be available. Neither will credit to start your own business. Your wages, if you have any, will be garnished leaving your employer less likely to consider you for advancement. When the time comes, you will not be able to co-sign loans so your own kids can go to college. The noose is tight: if you can't repay your loan, you can't make the money you need to repay your loan.

You are, in effect, in a debtors' prison without walls, and millions of others are in there with you. The restrictions on your personal economic activity mean the entire economy is hurt. You will never realize your full potential no matter what your qualifications or ability, both because of the exploitive nature of the loans you were given and because you graduated from college at a time when our evolving economy can no longer provide good-paying entry-level jobs. Joseph Stiglitz, winner of the Noble Prize in economics, put it this way, "…data show very clearly that if a young person graduates from college in a period in which there's high unemployment, the income prospect for your entire life is going to be greatly diminished."

The problem, unfortunately, does not stop with the individuals who borrowed the money. It can also impact their families. If a student loan is co-signed by a family member, and that loan goes into default, the co-signer becomes fully liable for the entire amount of the loan. He or she is also denied bankruptcy protection. If these family members cannot keep up with the required loan repayments, their wages can be garnished, their credit corrupted, and their economic potential limited. Their assets are even subject to seizure. Indeed, some have lost homes through a forced sale or foreclosure.

As a result, some former students forced to default on their loans have become responsible for the financial ruin of their families simply because their families tried to help them go to college.

During the decade leading up to the financial collapse in 2008, banks significantly increased demands that family members co-sign private student loans. The Consumer Financial Protection Bureau states that by 2005, 55% of such loans had a co-signer. At that point, the trend dramatically accelerated, and by 2011, 90% of private student loans had co-signers.

This is critically important for future as well as past borrowers. The ever-rising cost of a college education means that even the students who receive federal loans in the future will still need a family member to co-sign a supplemental private bank loan because the federal loan will not be large enough to cover all their expenses. Those who do not qualify for federal loans at all will be entirely dependent on private bank loans. Family members will have to either co-sign a student loan or take out a non-educational loan on their own credit. Either way, the entire family's finances will be placed at risk.

The demand for co-signers has bizarre consequences. If a student's parents are still paying off their own student loans or for some other reason are not sufficiently credit-worthy to co-sign a new loan, grandparents often have to step into the breech. If after graduating the student becomes unemployed and has to default on the loan, the co-signing grandparent has to make the required monthly payments. If she is unable, her pensions and social security checks can be garnished even if she has no other source of support.

This is not a small problem. The U.S. Treasury's Financial Management Service reports roughly 24,000 social security recipients who had a portion of their benefits garnished in 2001 to cover defaulted student loans. By 2007, that figure had increased to 60,000, and by late 2012, it was up to 119,000 and continuing to rise.

These numbers result from defaults, but the inter-generational impact of the student loan crisis can also be seen in those loans that are being paid off on time. In 2012, the Federal Reserve Bank of New York reported roughly 2.2 million people 60 years of age or older paying off student loans they had co-signed or direct loans made for educational expenses. In 2007, this group only owed $15 billion on such loans, but five years later, in 2012, that figure had almost tripled to roughly $43 billion.

The Federal Reserve also looked at total installment debt for people between 65 and 74. In 2007, they found that the portion related to educational loans was too low to include in their report. By 2010, only three years later, the portion of total installment debt being paid for educational loans in that age cohort had shot up to 13%.

Not only can pension and social security payments be garnished to pay off defaulted student loans, so can disability checks. A *Rolling Stone* article in 2013 described a previously healthy attorney in his late 30s who had suffered a catastrophic illness and become disabled. Bed-ridden and immobilized, he went into debt and had to default on his student loan. He soon qualified for federal disability, but once he did the federal Department of Education garnished $170 per month from his disability payments to pay down his student loan. It is hard to imagine a more appropriate candidate for bankruptcy protection, but that protection was not available.

Even death will not satisfy the banks. Federal student loans are forgiven at death, but private bank loans are not. In June 2012, *Propublica.org* told the moving story of a gardener whose son was killed in an auto accident shortly after graduating college. As the father grieved, he had to fend off bill collectors. The bank that had given his son a student loan, which he had co-signed, insisted on repayment. The gardener's annual income of $21,000 had to support the rest of his small family, but for years those bill collectors continued to hound him. At the time of the report, he was still at their mercy: another perfect candidate for bankruptcy protection.

The pain and suffering that result from defaulted or delinquent educational loans is no longer limited to the students doing the borrowing. Instead, the student loan crisis has become a metastasizing cancer that has spread to other generations and created cascading effects that damage people who have never set foot in a college classroom.

That damage impacts future generations. If student debt leaves a person unable or less able to send their own children to college, the lives of those children will be diminished. They, too, might languish in dead-end jobs without pensions, medical benefits, or sick leave. Their own children will be more likely to end up deprived of the health and financial security as well as the material benefits that all Americans have come to expect. These are class divisions in our society, divisions that were once more permeable, but now are rigid and difficult to overcome.

Rigid class lines are the enemy of democracy. They tend to become more permanent over time. For example, the wealthy don't need student loans. They can enrich the lives of their children with lessons, travel, and private schools, giving them a competitive advantage. Later, influential friends can help those children land the few good jobs available. If the wealthy have a leg up in a competitive society like ours, everyone else has less of a chance to succeed. Poor and middle class students are forced to compete on a playing field tilted against them, and even if they do everything right, it is likely to not be enough.

The student loan crisis underscores an old truth about what happens in a market economy when government fails to protect the interests of working people: the rich get richer and the poor get poorer. The student loan crisis also demonstrates a new truth about America: we are losing our claim to be the land of opportunity. In fact, many countries now offer substantially greater opportunity to their young people, with or without a college education, than we do.

The root cause of the crisis over student loans is the high cost of college. We will not be able to reverse the downward trend in economic opportunities for young people until we find a better way to finance their education. Asking college students to mortgage their futures with huge student loans and begin their fragile economic lives weighted down by a mountain of debt is not a credible strategy for rebuilding our economy. Why then did the cost of college go up so dramatically, and why did it rise faster than the cost of everything (literally, *everything*) else.

Chapter 3: How Did College Tuition Become So Expensive?

The student loan crisis is a new phenomenon. Despite its huge impact, as recently as the late 1980s there was no student loan crisis. Then, middle and working class students suffered from cutbacks and had difficulty financing their educations, but overall, while the system of paying for college was beginning to break down, it had not yet become the disaster it is today. The crisis came because in later years the cost of getting a higher education rose many times faster than the overall cost of living. To make matters worse, wages were stagnant and the real purchasing power of working Americans was in decline.

The crisis now centers on the inability of borrowers to repay their student loans, but those borrowers only needed loans in the first place because in the mid-1990s the cost of tuition escalated so dramatically. By the first decade of the new century, it virtually went through the roof. What drove this sudden and rapid increase?

When I was a young man in the late 1950s, many families could afford college even though far fewer than today thought it necessary. The son or daughter of a working class family could attend a public college or university where the cost of tuition was almost negligible, even for families with limited funds. Working class kids with enough talent could win scholarships to attend the more elite private universities, as I did. But even those private universities kept tuition low enough for middle class families to afford. I used my scholarship at the University of Chicago, one of the most expensive institutions in the country. Tuition was $870 per year when I enrolled in 1958 (just under $7,000 in 2013 dollars).

Young people in my time had access to an additional advantage students are unlikely to have today: part-time jobs during the school year and full-time temporary jobs in the summer. The extra money allowed me to pay for my own living expenses and graduate without debt and without having burdened my parents. I was typical. The robust American economy at the time allowed many students like me to "work our way through college." That phrase sounds quite hollow today since most of those jobs no longer exist.

For the 20 years prior to the mid-1980s, college tuition rose only gradually. Middle class families had come to understand that a degree meant greater earning power. Their children flocked to college and quickly increased total enrollment from 8.5 million in 1970 to 13.8 million in 1990. Campuses had to expand to meet the new demand. As a result, tuition increased at a rate somewhat greater than the increase in the overall cost of living. Nevertheless, the situation remained stable since costs were not going up fast enough to trigger changes in the way higher education was financed. That was no longer true by the late-1980s, when tuition began to increase at a rate faster than the overall cost of living.

That dramatic increase occurred because during this period many states developed large budget deficits. In the late 1980s and 1990s these budget deficits increased because of popular support for tax-cutting measures at all levels of government. To give voters lower taxes, states had to reduce public services. Welfare and poverty programs were cut first, but more cuts were necessary to keep the deficits under control.

Legislators tried to preserve their state college and university budgets for reasons of pride and prestige, but the budget ax soon fell on them as well. When state appropriations for these campuses were cut, college administrators had no choice but to raise tuition to make up for the shortfalls.

To understand the nationwide impact of these budget-driven tuition increases at state colleges and universities consider the fact that 80% of all American students enrolled in degree-granting, non-profit institutions attend publicly funded colleges and universities. The tuition increases at these public institutions directly affected the overwhelming majority of American students.

With the budget cuts temporarily neutralized by tuition increases, college administrators saw the expanding student population (the market for their services) as an opportunity to enlarge the size and standing of their campuses. Universities competed for prominent faculty by offering larger salaries. They expanded and modernized their laboratory space to attract prestigious government grants. New sports facilities were built along with dormitories that advertised comforts unheard of when I was a student. Some schools, to their credit, responded to the growing demand for fairness by offering more scholarships to disadvantaged students. All of these factors played a role in increasing the cost of tuition, but the main reason it went up was that legislative appropriations for higher education went down.

Cuts in these appropriations got worse in the 1990s, and then plummeted even further during the following decade. That drove tuition up to previously unheard of levels. The result was a tectonic shift in American higher education: instead of the states taking primary responsibility for the cost of higher education, the expense was gradually transferred to the students.

Here's an example. By 1990, Ohio had already cut back its funding for public higher education. That year the state's flagship university, Ohio State, received only 25% of its budget from the legislature, necessitating another tuition increase. Ten years later, in 2000, state allocations for the school had been reduced to only 15% of overall costs. In 2012, Ohio State received a mere 7% of its funds from the State of Ohio. Tuition over that interval increased accordingly.

The situation in Ohio was not unique. Across the country, the *Seattle Times* reported that tuition at the University of Washington had increased by 150% over the ten years between 2003 and 2013, five times the rate of inflation. The blame is laid on sharp state budget cutbacks. In 2003, Washington State funded 64% of the university's budget. In 2013 that figure had been reduced to 31%. Alarming as these cutbacks are, comparable reductions in state funding are not limited to Ohio and Washington. Nor have they run their course.

State university budget cuts continue today and are accelerating. The Center on Budget and Policy Priorities looked at the years since the start of the 2008 recession. Their findings are startling. As low as state budgets for higher education were in 2008, states in 2013 planned to spend 28% less per student. At the same time, state tuition has gone up an average of 27% over that same, very limited, period.

Looking just at the years between 2007 and 2012, tuition at public four-year colleges has gone up by more than 15% in 40 states, more than 25% in 18 states, and more than 50% in seven states. California and Arizona increased their public university tuition by more than 70% between 2007 and 2012.

Across all public institutions of higher education in the nation in 2011-12, state funds appropriated for colleges and universities fell by a staggering 7.6% – in a single year! The Center for the Study of Education Policy claims that is the largest annual drop in half a century. Cuts like these are the engine driving the tuition increases that have completely reshaped the American educational landscape.

When the public universities increased their tuition, the elite private universities took notice. Anxious to maintain their higher status and simultaneously bring in more revenue, they raised their tuition as well, setting off an escalating spiral. The result is visible today in the eye-popping tuition rates that now confront students at private colleges and universities. At my old school, the University of Chicago, entering students in 2013 paid $44,574 for tuition and fees. Room, board and books required another $14,446. The escalation of these costs is certain to continue. The big name private schools turn away 75% or more of their applicants. They have no reason to lower tuition and every reason to continue raising it.

In the three decades between 1980 and 2010, the United States underwent a sea change in how it finances higher education. The Consumer Price Index over that period roughly doubled, meaning that most things cost about twice what they did 30 years earlier. Many are aware that over the same period the cost of health care did not just double but increased six times over what it had been. Few Americans, however, realize that during that same period the cost of college tuition went up twice as fast as the cost of health care. Add the disappearance of part-time and temporary summer jobs for college students and the implications for higher education are clear: in three decades the cost of college rose from relatively accessible to shockingly unaffordable.

Those three decades also witnessed radically widening disparities between working and middle class families on the one hand and wealthy families on the other. The Economic Policy Institute found that between 1978 and 2011, roughly the same three decades, average CEO salaries increased by 725%. Workers' salaries over the same period increased less than 6%. Taking a longer view, they showed that in 1960 the top 1% of income earners in the U.S. collectively made 8.4% of the total income generated in the country. Fifty years later, in 2010, the top 1% had doubled their take to 17.4% of total income.

As the purchasing power of working and middle class families declined, college was seen as ever more necessary in the desperate struggle for financial success. But rapidly rising tuition made college less and less affordable. Trapped between their perceived need for an education and their lack of resources with which to pay for it, many families had no choice but to seek larger and larger student loans.

Chapter 4: Why Are Student Loans So Biased In Favor of the Banks?

The student loan system was so poorly designed that the loans it generated were doomed to become unfair and exploitive. Over time the cards became so stacked against the borrowers that the banks were able to gather up all the chips. The system's evolution into the full-blown disaster it is today reveals a great deal about how our government operates and the priorities that influence its actions.

The story begins on an October day in 1957. Much to the surprise of American military and political leaders, on that day the USSR launched the first earth-orbiting satellite, *Sputnik*. If the Russians had beaten us to space, they must also have superior intercontinental ballistics missiles. To calm widespread panic over a feared "missile gap," vast sums were pumped into the already swelled Cold War defense budget. But much of the blame for the "gap" fell on American education. We were behind in scientific training, not producing enough scientists, engineers and mathematicians to compete with the Russians.

Up to that point, aside from the G.I. Bill that sent many World War II veterans to college, there had never been federal scholarships or loans for college students. But soon after *Sputnik* was launched Congress passed the National Defense Education Act, which gave federal aid to public and private institutions at all grade levels with an emphasis on the hard sciences and foreign languages.

Other programs quickly followed, including low-interest loans to qualified students and later a small program that for the first time gave grants to needy students. The big breakthrough came in 1965 with passage of the Higher Education Act, wide-ranging legislation that authorized federal scholarships and provided federal guarantees for student loans.

What followed was a golden age for American higher education. Over the next two decades, legislatures generously supported state colleges and universities. Governments at all levels provided scholarships and favorable loans. College students were seen as the future leaders of society, and opportunities were created for them commensurate with such hopes. Upon graduation, good-paying entry-level jobs and the absence of debt allowed young people to get a head start toward fulfilling careers. Higher education became an effective ladder for class mobility, just as so many hopeful parents thought it would.

The Higher Education Act of 1965, part of President Johnson's War on Poverty, has been amended numerous times and remains operational today. But buried within it is a grievous error that undermined its intent in later decades. Instead of using the federal government's own dollars to dramatically expand student loan programs, Congress allowed banks to make the loans using their cash with the government guaranteeing repayment, that is, if the student was unable to repay the bank, the government would.

This peculiar arrangement allowed government to argue that it had created a win-win situation. The banks would profit and the students would get interest rates slightly below market. It also allowed Congress to keep the loans off the federal books, which was important because the war in Viet Nam had begun to strain the budget. It was poor accounting but it seemed like good politics. It wasn't. Their decision gradually gave rise to a new student loan business run by the nation's banks.

By the middle of the 1980s, the golden age of American higher education had lost its luster as tuition slowly increased. In the 1990s, it faded further when the cost of a college education rose to levels that required large student loans. After 2000, the golden age turned into a nightmare because college costs had escalated so rapidly that loans of disastrous proportions were required. Then the good post-graduation jobs disappeared and millions were left unable to repay their loans.

Changes in the American economy during the same period deserve part of the blame. Fewer tax dollars were available for public services, and wealth and income shifted to the upper classes. But those changes don't tell the whole story. When government first gave control of student loans to the banks in 1965, it created a new business, one required by the laws of commerce to focus on maximizing its profits rather than helping its needy student customers. Operations were relatively benign at first, but when tuition dramatically escalated, the huge profit potential of the student loan business became clear to the bankers.

Here's how the system worked. If the federally guaranteed student loans were repaid, the banks kept the fees and interest that had been charged during the life of the loan. If the loans were not repaid, the government not only covered the banks' losses but also their late fees and penalties. The banks couldn't lose. They were required to charge fixed interest at somewhat less than market rates, but the rates were still far too high and capable of generating huge profits.

Since their money was never at risk, a reasonable person might ask why the banks were not required to provide students with non-profit interest rates or rates significantly below the market. A good question, but one that escaped the attention of the politicians who approved this system in 1965. Through the federal guarantees on these student loans, the government gave the banking industry an undeserved and unearned windfall.

The banks quickly found other ways to generate more profit. Because there were not enough federal loans for all the students who needed them, and because the federal loans were not large enough to cover all expenses, the banks went into the additional business of providing private educational loans, often with the assistance of college administrators who steered new students to them.

For these private student loans, the banks were able to charge even higher interest rates, as well as ignore various consumer loan protections. Many students ended up with multiple loans at varying interest rates. The banking industry had every reason to be pleased with these arrangements and lobbied Congress to expand federal student loan programs. As tuition kept increasing and larger loans became a necessity, the banks ended up in the driver's seat. They then used their influence with Congress to make sure they stayed there.

During the late 1980s and early 1990s, with tighter federal budgets, federal aid to needy students failed to keep up with the expanding college population and the increasing cost of a college education. President Reagan and the first President Bush were elected on the basis of promises to lower taxes. That also led them to cut the number of students eligible for federal loans, reduce interest subsidies on federal loans, and lower the levels of direct assistance to low-income students receiving grants.

President Clinton took office in 1993 and quickly realized that having the banks put up the money for federal loans hurt both students and taxpayers. If the loan money came directly from the Treasury, he argued, taxpayers would no longer be stuck with the bank fees, and the banks trying to collect on their loans would no longer be able to mistreat students, as many of them had done. At first, Congress agreed with Clinton, a Democrat, but when Newt Gingrich led a Republican takeover of the House of Representatives in 1995, Clinton's idea was pushed aside and direct loans from the Treasury became only a small part of the federal student loan program.

Three years later, in 1998, Congress, still under Gingrich's control, had to once again reauthorize the 1965 Higher Education Act. They attached an amendment that came to have a profound impact on future students, an impact that led directly to some of the worst aspects of the student loan crisis.

For the first time, those with federally guaranteed student loans would no longer have the right to discharge their loans through bankruptcy. That amendment would keep borrowers on the hook permanently and allow the banks to collect even more unearned and undeserved income in fees, penalties and interest. Never before had the government singled out a class of legal loans and repealed the right of borrowers to discharge them through bankruptcy.

During the years leading up to 1998, a wave of deregulation had engulfed the federal government. Many laws regulating and limiting the behavior of businesses, especially in the banking and finance sectors, were repealed or severely weakened. Conservative political analysis, dominant at the time, viewed these laws as needlessly interfering with private enterprise and unjustifiably extending federal powers.

The deregulation conservatives supported profoundly enriched and empowered the banking industry. When they had realized that legislation of this sort could be easily won by making large contributions to key politicians, the bankers had refocused their attention on Washington. Previously, they had given the bulk of their financial support to Republicans, but once he was in the White House, they also threw their weight behind Bill Clinton and other Democrats. Their efforts paid off in 1998 when Clinton signed the amendment removing bankruptcy protection from federal student loans. Soon, millions of student borrowers were condemned to new financial hardships, and some to out-right financial ruin.

Bankruptcy is a form of debt forgiveness, an issue that has plagued societies since the dawn of civilization. Moses called for a "jubilee" every fifty years to wipe away all debts. In ancient Greece, debtors were forced into slavery with their family members and household servants until the debt was worked off. In colonial times, Americans unable to pay creditors could be put in debtors' prisons.

American bankruptcy laws were not fully codified until the Great Depression. The U.S. Supreme Court set down our fundamental approach to the problem in 1934. Bankruptcy laws, they stated, give "…to the honest but unfortunate debtor…a new opportunity in life and clear field for future effort, unhampered by the pressure and discouragement of preexisting debt." The Justices stated that the main purpose of a bankruptcy was to give people with impossible debt burdens a "fresh start."

Banks make two sorts of loans, secured and unsecured. With secured loans, like home mortgages and automobile financing, the lender can seize the property (the home or car) that secures the loan if the borrower is unable to repay. With unsecured loans, like credit cards, borrowers unable to repay their loans because of profound and insoluble economic problems can declare bankruptcy and have a court verify their inability to pay. If the court agrees, their debt is cancelled and they get a "fresh start."

Bankers have to live with this possibility, and if it happens, absorb the loss. It is for taking this "risk" that capitalism justifies the interest rates charged on loans. Naturally, if a new law significantly lowers risk, as when bankruptcy protection was removed from federal student loans, it follows that the beneficiaries, in this case the banks, will make more money and should be forced to compensate, for example, by lowering interest rates. Law and logic both dictate that government should not pass legislation that give unfair advantage to some citizens at the expense of others. You would think such logic would have applied to student loans. It didn't.

Originally, all federal student loans were eligible for bankruptcy protection. But after the oil embargo and recession in the mid-1970s, Congress took steps to shore up the weakening economy. Included was legislation that prevented student borrowers from using bankruptcy protection for a minimum of five years after their repayments began. Later, that interval was extended to seven years.

In 1997, Congress appointed a commission to review growing problems with the nation's bankruptcy laws. The commission recommended, among other proposals, that all student loans be fully dischargeable via bankruptcy. Instead of accepting that advice, Congress did the opposite. Encouraged by the bankers, they passed the 1998 amendment that ended bankruptcy protection for federal students loans.

It was an undeserved and unnecessary slap in the face to students who were then being pounded by rapidly escalating tuition costs. With exceedingly rare exceptions, students in 1998 did not borrow money expecting to be so unemployable after graduation as to be unable to repay their loans. At that time, there were still reasonably good job prospects for college graduates. Instead, the new law depriving student borrowers of bankruptcy protection was simply a present Congress gift-wrapped for the banks.

The 1998 amendments were a milestone. For the first time, the federal government sanctioned the naked exploitation of college students. The only other loans for which bankruptcy protection is not available are those involved with criminal, illegal, or intentionally harmful behavior. The loss of bankruptcy protection for federal student loans meant that the government would pay the banks for the fees, penalties and compound interest generated by the defaulted loans, while at the same time maintaining the guarantee on the original amount borrowed.

Essentially, the government had passed a law that gave the banks a massive uncompensated financial gift. Ironically, it was a gift that violated the fundamental laws of the free market and therefore of capitalism itself. Adding to the irony, the law was pushed hardest by the very same conservative politicians who had all but deified free market policies.

Unfortunately, an even bigger outrage was still in the future. The 1998 amendment removed bankruptcy protection from federally guaranteed student loans, loans in which the federal government actually had a financial interest. In 2005, Congress, still under Republican control and supported by the second President Bush, removed the right to bankruptcy for student loans obtained from private banks, loans in which the government had no financial interest whatsoever.

No other borrowers have ever been subjected to a comparable loss of rights, and no lenders have ever been awarded such protection. This decision turned the principles of capitalism on their head, but no cries of outrage were heard on Wall Street. It was, after all, a present to an industry that had been heavily funding both political parties in order to win exactly such advantage. And so arrogant were the bankers, so politically unassailable, that no one in government even suggested that this gift should be compensated by a forced reduction in the interest rates paid by student borrowers.

The 2005 loss of bankruptcy protection for private student loans was followed by more government discrimination. Student borrowers lost a variety of consumer protections, including truth-in-lending laws and safeguards against usury. Guidelines that had previously limited the behavior of unscrupulous debt collectors were removed – provided the debt collectors were in pursuit of ex-students. The wages of student borrowers, unlike others, became subject to garnishment without legal hearings. Meanwhile, government continued to cut the size and availability of federal student loans, which forced even more students, either in desperation or confusion, to seek higher interest loans from private banks.

Some of these banks were not satisfied with merely exploiting the students. They began to actively cheat the government. Functioning as a private bank, Sallie Mae, originally a government-sponsored entity, made numerous federally guaranteed student loans. If these loans default, the government pays the bank a 120% recovery along with all fees and penalties due. Sallie Mae filed numerous claims seeking such reimbursement for student loans it claimed were in default, but when federal investigators looked into the matter they discovered that the bank had made no effort to collect on the loans. That year Sallie Mae paid $3.4 million in fines to avoid further prosecution.

Government had created a system so biased in favor of the banks that Sallie Mae and others engaged in similar swindles found it more profitable to make fraudulent recovery claims than to actually try to collect the student loans they had made, which remained protected by the federal guarantees. Two years later, Sallie Mae admitted that a substantial portion of their record-breaking profits had come from federal reimbursement for defaulted student loans. An outraged Congress should have forced them out of business. But Congress was too busy facilitating such activities, and so in 2004 Sallie Mae transformed itself into an entirely private bank. Not only did it survive, by 2013 it was the largest private lender of high interest student loans.

Chapter 5: How It All Came Together To Hurt Students

In the mid-1980s, the cost of college began to rise much faster than the rate of inflation. That forced an ever-increasing number of students to borrow money. By 1992, 45% of college students found it necessary to take out a loan. But in the late 1990s and the first decade of the new century college costs increased even faster, eventually at many times the overall rate of inflation. The result, by 2007, was that 67% of college students had loans.

Imagine what that meant to the bankers. In less than 50 years, they had created a new business that had turned two-thirds of the nation's approximately 20 million college students into paying customers. They did this without marketing expenses or having to take significant risk. Every year they got another million or so new customers without spending a dime on advertising, while their old customers continued to rack up new interest charges and supply them with a massive stream of new cash. The bankers had turned American college kids into their own private ATM. It was all too good to be true.

Meanwhile, the same banks that were in the student loan business were also making home loans, and doing so as fast as they could write the paper, paying little heed to the ability of borrowers to repay. Soon, the massive number of their irresponsible home loans fueled the Great Recession of 2008. The story of how the reckless behavior of the banking industry crashed the entire economy has been told many times.

Less well known is the fact that the banks applied identical practices to the private student loans they were writing, the loans not backed by federal guarantees.

These loans generally came with high interest rates, and as tuition increases forced more students to use them, the banks began an orgy of lending comparable to but not as widespread as their mortgage lending. They gave money to student borrowers who did not fully understand the terms of their loans and who could not afford the amounts they were given. Many of these excessive private bank loans now make up the defaulted and delinquent loans that are the most painful part of the student loan crisis.

Similar to the housing crisis, this excessive lending was fueled by Wall Street investor demands for asset-backed securities. The banks bundled the student loans and resold them in the same way they packaged and resold home mortgages. Collectively, these loans amounted to $5 billion in 2001, but in the frenzy leading up to the crash in 2008, they increased to about $20 billion annually and made their own small contribution to the Great Recession.

Back in 2006, the federal government had given another gift to the banking industry when it set the interest on federally guaranteed bank loans (as well as the few available direct federal loans) at a fixed rate of 6.8%. This was touted as a break for students, but it allowed the banks to earn much higher profits than they deserved given that the loans were guaranteed and had no risk.

The 6.8% loans would either be repaid with interest by the student borrowers or the government would give the banks a 120% settlement on any loans in default. This gift to the banks became immensely more valuable after the 2008 recession, when the interest rates banks paid to borrow money from the Federal Reserve tumbled to near zero. With students still paying them 6.8% on loans guaranteed by the government, this taxpayer subsidized break for the "too big to fail" banks was not passed along to students. The banks realized two more years of huge windfall profits.

In response to this glaring inequity, two changes were made. First, after the recession, Congress passed legislation that very gradually lowered the student loan interest rate to 3.4% by the 2012-2013 academic year. Second, in 2010, President Obama finally ended the 45-year mistake of allowing private banks to front the money for federally guaranteed student loans. After 2010, federal student loans came out of the Treasury, which meant no more 120% reimbursement, fraudulent default claims or guaranteed profits for the banks, although all of these deficiencies remained in place for federal loans made prior to 2010. Because the new federal loans came from the Treasury, the government was able to set new repayment schedules that took the borrower's income, or lack of income, into consideration.

The law lowering student loan interest rates to 3.4% was due to expire in 2013. As that date approached, Democrats and Republicans in Congress debated plans to extend the low rate but were unable to agree. As a result, the rate doubled back to the original 6.8% in June 2013. The resulting public outrage was so intense that Congress finally reached a settlement. In August 2013 President Obama signed new legislation linking student loan interest rates to the 10-year Treasury bond rate.

Tying the interest rate on federal student loans to the Treasury bond rate was at least a step in the right direction. Interest rates that students pay the federal government for money they borrow should be related to the interest rates that the federal government has to pay for the money it borrows. (Treasury bonds are essentially money the government borrows from bond purchasers; the Treasury bond rate is the interest the government has to pay to borrow that money.)

However, while the Treasury bond rate and the interest on student loans were linked, they did not become equal. Under this law, students receiving new federal loans will pay an interest rate equal to the Treasury bond rate, whatever it is at the time, plus a fixed percentage, 2.05% for college students and 3.60% for graduate students. It is estimated at the time of this writing that with current Treasury bond rates fluctuating between 2% and 3%, college students will have to pay an interest rate between 4% and 5% through the 2015 academic year.

There is much that is wrong with this new system. Tying interest rates to fluctuating Treasury bond rates means that federal student loans will have variable interest rates, that is, if the cost of borrowing money increases for the government (reflected in increased Treasury bond rates), their added costs will be passed on to students in the form of escalating interest rates on their existing student loans.

This new arrangement means that students will be unable to effectively calculate how much to borrow based on how much they think they will be able to repay because the amount they will owe will depend on these fluctuating interest rates. When the government borrows money by selling Treasury bonds, it fixes the interest rate for the life of the bond. If the government is willing to sell Treasury bonds at a fixed rate, there is no reason for it to insist that students pay a variable rate.

But a far more serious flaw is that this new system sets student loan interest rates so high that now the federal government instead of the banks will be making huge profits on student loans. Government's initial profits came in the period after 2010 but before 2013 when the new legislation tying federal student loan interest rates to the 10-year Treasury bond rate took effect. This was the period when interest rates on student loans were gradually falling from 6.8% in 2008 to 3.4% in 2013. The 10-year Treasury bond rate at this time averaged about 2%.

It may appear that the difference between what the government was paying to borrow money (about 2%) and what it was charging to lend money (that plus 2.05% for college students and 3.60% for graduate students) was trivial, but that small difference was enough to generate massive profits. Because government profits are subject to public disclosure, we know that the Department of

Education booked student loan profits of roughly $48 billion in 2011, about $28 billion in 2012, and over $42 billion in 2013. By way of comparison, Exxon Mobil, the most profitable private corporation in the world, had profits of about $45 billion in 2012.

Instead of being fleeced by the banks, students during these years were fleeced by the government. The federal government earning multi-billion dollar profits on student loans is an outrage. It's the equivalent of a special tax on the students and families who can least afford college, those forced to borrow to attend.

Advocates for students had hoped that after 2010 the government would lend money to college students on a non-profit basis. The best way to do that, from the students' perspective, would be for the government to borrow money from the Federal Reserve at the discount rate, the rate the Fed charges for lending money to major banks, and offer that rate, which is lower than the Treasury bond rate, to students. Prior to the recession, the discount rate was about 5%. After the recession it was reduced to near zero to stimulate the economy, and as of early 2014, it remained at 0.75%.

In 2013, newly elected Sen. Elizabeth Warren wrote a bill that tied future federal student loan interest rates to the Fed's discount rate. Her bill had so little support, it failed to get out of committee. There is virtually no chance that such legislation will be passed in the foreseeable future. Without it, the federal government will join the banks in the ongoing exploitation of America's student population.

The scope of that exploitation is startling. In August 2013, the Congressional Budget Office (CBO) completed a 10-year projection of student loan profits. Including losses it forecast for the years between 2014 and 2016, the CBO estimated that between 2013 and 2023, the federal government would make a profit of $184 billion from its student loan program. Hopefully, even those who object to a non-profit system will admit that government has no business making profits of that magnitude on the backs of college students.

Understand that the $184 billion in government profits over that ten-year period is nowhere near the total profit that will be made from student loans. It only reflects profits that will be made on federal student loans, not private student loans from banks. Federal student loans are only granted to a portion of the total student population, and they rarely cover all of a student's expenses. As a result, more and more students are driven into the waiting arms of the banks, which remain free to make private loans at interest rates higher than the federal loans.

The projection of $184 billion in government profit over the next ten years can be taken as a yardstick of profits generated for the banks by federal student loans over the past ten years. Given the higher interest rates that prevailed, the banks must have made at least that much and probably more. A comparable or perhaps slightly smaller amount was likely made during the ten years before that. Once again, these profits do not include what the banks made on their private loans, nor do they include the windfall profits realized in 2009 and 2010.

The conclusion is inescapable. Over the past few decades, the student loan system probably resulted in the transference of somewhere between $500 and $800 billion from working and middle class families to the nation's biggest banks. This enormous blow was delivered on top of the damage already done to those families by the declining manufacturing economy and the 2008 recession.

Remarkably, this vast transfer of wealth is only rarely cited as a cause of the extreme income and wealth inequality that currently plagues our country and undermines our economy. With so many hundreds of billions moving from working and middle class families to Wall Street banks, there can be little doubt that the student loan swindle played a major role, and will continue to do so.

What does all this mean for people holding private bank loans and pre-2010 federal student loans? Very little. The public controversies, the government debates, the proposed solutions, are all focused on future federal borrowers. No one is seriously addressing the loans made in the past, federal or private, and the myriad problems those loans cause in the present. Nonetheless, this lengthy description of the controversies surrounding future loans should make it clear that the federal government cannot be relied upon to defend the interests of America's college students, past, present or future.

The 2008 recession hit those students like a perfect storm, leaving them swamped or underwater. The recession taught us, first, that the American system of higher education can no longer be sustained. The massive tuition increases and the resulting need for equally massive student loans are one problem, but when that problem is combined with the loss of entry-level jobs that ex-students need to repay their loans, it forces large numbers of borrowers into default. Remember the job statistics cited at the beginning of Chapter 2: slightly more than half of college graduates in 2012 were unemployed, under-employed or working in unpaid internships.

The recession also taught us that the removal of bankruptcy protection was the key factor in creating this public policy disaster. Student borrowers with no financial resources and no employment prospects are exactly the kind of people that bankruptcy is supposed to protect – but these students can't get a "fresh start," the purpose of bankruptcy, because the federal government denied them a protection available on all other legitimate loans.

The loan defaults that have occurred in the absence of bankruptcy were followed by even more punishment: the inability to meaningfully participate in the economy – no credit, no business loans, garnished wages, no means to buy a home or a car, no ability to attend graduate school. It was the loss of bankruptcy protection on student loans that condemned part of an entire generation to ruin of this sort.

Finally, the 2008 recession taught us that the problems associated with the student loan crisis are not episodic, that is, they are not temporary aberrations in our economy likely to disappear in the next cycle of prosperity, if indeed there is one. Our overall economy is in decline. The recession, coupled with that decline, means reduced tax revenue for the states, which will lead to more cuts in state budgets for higher education and greater pressure on public universities to raise tuition. When they do, the private universities will follow.

This is an unstable situation that is going to get worse. Reduced economic activity will make good jobs even harder to find, and pay, already going down, will decrease further. The Bureau of Labor Statistics states that median weekly wages for people with Bachelors degrees fell 4.8% (inflation adjusted) between 2003 and 2013. Even singling out those over 25 who hold college degrees, wages over the same period were down 3%.

Ironically, such decreases in earning power make it even more important to obtain a college degree since those without one earn even less, far less. Future students will have no choice but to swallow the coming tuition increases and apply for even larger loans. When they graduate, many will join the ranks of the unemployed, which will put added pressure on the jobs market. That paradoxically will drive even more students to seek the presumed but diminishing advantages of a college degree. It will be a downward spiral that will worsen every year.

Given that federal loan programs are limited both in the size of the loans and the number of loans available, students will increasingly be forced into oppressive loan contracts with private banks. And with the banks now requiring family members to co-sign almost all of their loans, non-students will be drawn into this expanding vortex of debt and pain.

Hard as it may be to believe, the full impact of the student loan crisis is not yet apparent. New problems will arise, and when they do, the new federal student loan programs will have to be continually fine-tuned. The energy and attention that will be required to do that will keep the focus on future student loans, where it is now. The student loan crisis of the past will be a decreasing priority, and the victims of the student loan swindle will be left behind once again.

These former students will only get relief if they take matters into their own hands. The banking industry has no desire to help; their interests lie in the opposite direction. Some in government genuinely want to help, but the forces arrayed against them are too powerful. They are likely to remain preoccupied with the more politically expedient task of defending current and future students.

When I attended college in the late 1950s and early 1960s, society paved our way to secure and productive lives with scholarships and affordable tuition. That was a reflection of the values prominent at the time: optimism about the future, faith in the expanding middle class, trust in education as a ladder of class mobility.

Today, those values have not been openly repudiated, but they no longer guide education policy. Instead, an oppressive system has evolved in which middle class kids spend their childhoods struggling to get into the right preparatory high schools – often starting with pre-school or kindergarten – while working class kids are rarely allowed to aspire to a first-rate college at all. Later, both will mortgage their uncertain futures and gamble that decent jobs will be there after graduation.

Government should have seen these problems coming and taken steps to prevent them. When student loans were first instituted in the 1960s, officials failed to think through the possible consequences. They inadvertently unleashed the greed of the banking industry, which then used its new wealth to influence subsequent government decisions, like the loss of bankruptcy protection. Instead of nurturing college students, government handed them over to bankers who saw them only as sheep to be shorn.

That initial mistake had little impact for the first twenty years of the federal student loan program. But when tuition rapidly increased, the bankers saw their opportunity and pounced. Government is supposed to be in the business of public service; banks are not. Their mission is to maximize their profits, and that's what they did. Student borrowers were seen only as customers willing to pay whatever the traffic would bear. They evolved from a population to be helped into one to be exploited. Then, when other factors drove the cost of higher education to astonishing heights requiring far larger loans, the profit that could be made from that exploitation rose to astronomical levels.

This massive public policy failure is part of an overall collapse of our enlightened self-interest.

Our society is so focused on the present and on near-term advantages that it is losing its ability to intelligently plan for the future. Instead, we are strip-mining that future. Youth is one of our most precious resources, but the system we have created wastes that resource for short-term gain instead of protecting it for the long run. What remains is a wasteland of lost potential.

Hope is not a strategy for change. In the case of the student loan crisis, with so many billions at stake, change will not come without a fight. Only those with enough skin in the game, those with private bank debt and the pre-2010 federal borrowers, can sustain a fight large enough and long enough to win. If you are one of them, your only chance is to combine with others in the same predicament and mount that fight. Without it, you will get no relief, while the banking industry and our misguided government continue to treat you and all of American youth as though you were just another domestic colony.

That may be a harsh description, but domestic colonies do exist. Latin American immigrants are one example. Paid less than others, their wages depress salaries for everyone else. My ancestors were welcomed to America and valued for what they and their descendants could contribute. Latin Americans are not. Working single moms are another domestic colony. Many are stuck in minimum wage jobs with no benefits, while their children receive sub-standard daycare. Society ignores the damage to those kids just as it condones the economic exploitation of their mothers. African Americans, of course, have a longer and deeper understanding of what it means to be stuck in a domestic colony.

The victims of the student loan crisis must either defend their own interests or be pushed down to similar status. If you are among them, your inability to start a new business, get additional job training, or buy a home or car is likely to push you farther and farther away from the prosperity you hoped to achieve by attaining a higher education.

Years ago, a college education was an effective ladder of social mobility. Through hard work and determination, many children of the working class did once qualify themselves for jobs that came with middle or even upper class advantages. Social mobility of that sort was so common it became enshrined in our collective mythology as "the American dream."

Now, such advancement is available to very few. A college education starts with the extraction of money from those students least able to afford it, the students who borrow thousands of dollars just to walk through the campus gate. College is no longer an engine for social advancement. In fact, it is now responsible for impoverishing rather than advancing many of its students. A system that funds higher education with massive student loans inevitably hardens class divisions and makes them even more unyielding and inflexible.

There are also damaging psychological aspects of the student loan crisis. Being deeply in debt is depressing and demoralizing. It promotes a self-loathing that leaves its victims less capable of resistance. If you are being impoverished by the student loan crisis, don't let that happen to you or your family. You have been ripped off, and you are still being ripped off. The proper response is anger, righteous anger, at those who did this to you.

Look around. See how many others are caught in the same trap. They are the allies with whom you can organize resistance, because blatant exploitation also comes with an inherent weakness: if the exploitation is too harsh, the exploited revolt.

Who then caused this rip-off? Who should be the target of your righteous anger?

Chapter 6: Who Is To Blame?

Declines in state tax revenue first forced legislators to cut higher education budgets. That led to tuition increases at the public colleges and universities, which in turn provoked tuition increases at private universities. This was the basic cause, both of the massive increase in the cost of higher education and the subsequent need for equally massive student loans.

But why did those state tax revenues decline in the first place? How did the banking industry, heavily regulated and controlled since the Great Depression, accumulate enough influence over the federal government to deprive student loans of bankruptcy protection? Why did the government ignore the plight of student borrowers in the years before the 2008 recession? The answers to these questions will point to the culprits who should be targeted.

When the federal government first launched aid to higher education in the late 1950s and early 1960s, we lived in an entirely different political era. Governments at all levels were still heavily influenced by the success of the New Deal programs that lifted our country out of the Great Depression in the 1930s.

Those programs pumped government money into the economy to create jobs and improve the lives of working people on the theory that "a rising tide lifts all boats," that is, if more people are employed at a living wage, there will be fewer people on welfare, more customers for the products and services the employees create, more tax money available to government to maintain the services it does provide, and more profits for business so they can expand and employ even more people.

This "liberal" approach to government remained dominant into the 1970s. Even a "conservative" Republican like Richard Nixon, who was elected president in 1968 (primarily because of the Viet Nam War), had no choice but to get behind liberal causes still popular with voters. Nixon advocated universal health care, signed the Clean Air and Clean Water Acts, and signed legislation creating the Environmental Protection Agency. No "conservative" or Republican candidate could advocate any of those positions today and survive politically. That's a good yardstick of how dramatically politics, especially Republican politics, has changed.

Throughout the 1970s, the liberal approach to government lost ground. The United States began a rapid and historic, even radical, shift in its prevailing ideology from liberal to conservative. That shift culminated in 1980 with the election of the Republican, Ronald Reagan, as president. The liberal pro-business consensus that had prevailed for the previous fifty years evaporated. Liberal ideas were abandoned and a persistent conservatism came to dominate the country, the culture, and the economy.

It should come as no surprise that the liberal ideas that lost favor in the 1970s did not go out of style by accident. They were pushed out. Corporate leaders had become increasingly outraged at limits imposed on their business practices by new federal initiatives like the Environmental Protection Agency and the Clean Air Act. They were also afraid that the new political movements of the 1960s signaled a rising progressivism that sought goals even farther to the left than the liberal policies of the day. Nor did they fail to notice that young people inspired by those movements were engaged in a new flirtation with socialism.

Corporate leaders launched a counter-offensive, both to affect the dominant culture and to win more influence and control over government. Throughout the 1970s, big corporations and wealthy conservatives funded new think tanks like the Heritage Foundation and the American Enterprise Institute, extended the reach of conservative publications, used new direct mail techniques to create conservative grassroots organizations like the Moral Majority, and dramatically expanded their trade associations. For example, during the 1970s the membership of the National Federation of Independent Business ballooned from 300 to 600,000.

This unprecedented expansion of conservative activism had a strong impact on the political culture of the nation. But conservative leaders were equally concerned about their impact and influence on congressional legislation. To that end, they built up their lobbying muscle. During the decade of the 1970s, the number of corporations represented by registered lobbyists in Washington increased from about 145 to roughly 2,400.

This major offensive by business leaders dovetailed with the development of a brilliant new political strategy. To back up Reagan's candidacy in 1980, conservatives campaigned on the slogan "Get government off our backs." In the years that followed, this galvanizing slogan became one of the great sleight-of-hand tricks in American political history.

The audacity was breathtaking. Instead of addressing the many problems emerging from American business practices and changes in the global economy, the conservative spotlight only illuminated the problems of government. They argued that taxes were too high, excessive regulation was strangling job creation, freeloaders were living off the welfare system, government employees were lazy, and government itself was inefficient and riff with corruption.

"Get government off our backs," provided a simple answer to a complex question: how had the post-war prosperity in the 1950s and 1960s morphed into an oil embargo in 1973, a worldwide recession that immediately followed, and the so-called economic "stag-flation" (stagnation and inflation unusually combined) of the Carter administration in the late 1970s.

The slogan was effective because it sounded plausible. It diverted attention from high unemployment, environmental pollution, corporate tax loopholes, staggering inflation, widespread discrimination, excessive oil profits, sweetheart defense contracts, lowering wages, and increasing retail energy costs, while simultaneously undermining the liberal reforms of the 1960s that conservatives had opposed all along.

So successful was this tactic that it has remained a cornerstone of conservative political strategy to this day. The cost, however, was great. The constant anti-government drumbeat undermined the confidence all Americans have in their government. Government service declined in prestige and government workers, often dedicated and hardworking, became undeserving targets of ridicule.

The diversionary slogan and the politics that flowed from it allowed Reagan and his followers to use government as a straw man. They made angry attacks on official waste and arrogant bureaucrats, which supported their arguments to defund government. They claimed that tax cuts for the rich would lead to a stronger economy. They cut poverty and welfare programs and reduced unemployment compensation and job training programs. Their policies made their politics perfectly clear. It was only the wealthy who benefited from the tax cuts and only the poor who suffered from the cutbacks.

When Reagan took office the top income tax bracket was 70%. When he left eight years later it was 28%. He lowered the capital gains tax rate and the corporate income tax rate, which also benefited the wealthy. At the same time, he worked to raise taxes on those earning less than $50,000 per year. Reagan justified his approach by claiming that tax breaks for the rich would "trickle down" to benefit the rest of us, a claim that turned out to be so wrong only the most diehard conservatives still make it today.

Reagan's spending cutbacks selectively impacted the poorer segments of society and the voting constituencies, like organized labor, that had opposed his election. Six months into his first term, Reagan refused to grant a wage increase to the nation's air traffic controllers. When they went out on strike, he fired them all and destroyed their union. That unleashed a larger anti-labor crusade that further reduced the influence of organized labor. Once strikes by autoworkers, steelworkers, or miners had been capable of bringing the entire national economy to a halt. After Reagan, that was no more.

But Reagan was not a traditional Republican. In fact, he turned Republican ideology upside down. He vastly increased military spending, which led to an even bigger federal budget than the one he had railed against as a candidate. Coupled with his tax cuts for the wealthy, those defense expenditures meant a vast increase in the deficit. Fiscal deficits had once been anathema to the Main Street politics of the Republican Party but were welcomed by the financiers on Wall Street who would profit from them, and who, as a result, significantly increased their financial commitment to the Republican Party.

The ensuing shift in Republican loyalty from Main Street to Wall Street produced significant change in corporate America. In place of the time-honored practice of reinvesting profits to slowly grow a company, profits were often used to increase executive compensation. Long-term investment gave way to a focus on short-term profit, on the next quarter's bottom line, which was the perspective of Wall Street and of shareholders. Not surprisingly, wealth was redistributed, and money filtered up to those already rich.

The enlarged federal deficits that resulted from Reagan's defense budget and tax cuts eventually forced cuts in federal programs that went beyond the poor and included, among others, college students. The number of students eligible for assistance was reduced, student loan interest subsidies were cut, student aid was scaled back, and eligibility for Pell Grants was limited. Students unable to gain access to federal loan programs that limited interest rates were driven into the waiting arms of the private banks that did not.

Reductions in federal assistance to students were justified by conservative political philosophy, which differed sharply from what had been the prevailing liberal approach. During the Johnson era in the 1960s, liberal Democrats controlled the White House and both branches of Congress. They viewed financial support for college students not only in the context of national defense but also as a way to achieve social and class mobility, allowing more working class kids to rise into middle class status and generate more wealth for society as a whole. Liberals believed that a good education would enable people to work more productively, earn more money, and be better insulated from the need for government assistance.

Conservatives, on the other hand, thought society could only be improved if individuals took responsibility for their own lives. Conservatives advocated a return to a culture of rugged individualism, where government would play a minimalist role and people would have to take care of themselves subject to the laws of the marketplace. They argued that a college education primarily benefits the individual being educated, not society at large. As a result, students, rather than government, should take responsibility for financing their own educations. This attitude both tolerated and justified the shift in the cost of higher education from the state to the student.

Reagan's election in 1980 coincided with a simultaneous Republican takeover of the US Senate, which lasted six years and facilitated the accomplishment of much of his agenda. It was strongly biased in favor of the rich, but that agenda did have a certain internal consistency. The call to reduce taxes appealed to a broad audience. At the same time, it required shrinking government services, which justified traditional opposition to such services by conservative Republicans. The fact that simultaneous and quite massive increases in defense spending were enlarging the government was conveniently overlooked. The resulting deficits were then used to justify more cuts in welfare spending. It was a tightly wrapped but internally consistent package.

At the same time, the cry of "get government off our backs" was used to undermine the controls that the federal government normally exercised over the behavior of the nation's largest corporations, including those in the upper reaches of finance. Reagan initiated a wave of government deregulation that gave large corporations, especially the big banks, more freedom from legal constraints. That added to their wealth and increased their ability to win additional concessions from government. A new period in the economic history of the nation began.

Previously, as a result of the Great Depression in the 1930s, government had instituted a wide variety of controls to limit certain business and banking practices and avoid another economic collapse. These were some of the regulations that corporate America targeted for repeal as they rebuilt their influence in the 1970s. When Reagan was elected along with a Republican Senate, he made the dismantling of those regulations a priority. Entire industries were profoundly changed, for example, the airline and telephone industries.

Deregulation continued after Reagan's departure in 1989. The groundwork he had laid during two terms shifted the nation from a fundamentally liberal philosophy of government to a fundamentally conservative one. Future presidents were compelled to conform to and extend this shift. Bill Clinton, the lone Democratic president in the 28 years between 1980 and 2008, was as limited by this conservative era as Richard Nixon had been by the liberal era just before. Clinton was also limited by the fact that in 1992 he was elected with only 43% of the vote due to the third party candidacy of Ross Perot, another indication of the national shift to conservatism.

In no sector of the economy did this shift have a greater impact on the economic future of the nation than in banking and finance. The twists and turns are too complex to explain here, but in the two decades that followed Reagan's terms in office, banking deregulation moved inexorably forward. With each step, Wall Street bankers not only improved their profits, they expanded their political power and then used it in Washington to win even more freedom from government regulation.

At the same time, thanks both to government tilting the playing field in favor of business and to the decreased influence of the labor movement, wages for working people declined, many of their benefits were lost, many of their jobs were sent overseas, and in general they had to work harder for less. The declining economic power of working and middle class families put a high premium on getting a college degree, despite the rapidly inflating cost. The banks were ready to take advantage of the new situation, and the student loan business mushroomed.

Eventually, the bankers' reckless lending behavior and credit abuses, freed from the usual constraints of regulation, resulted in the Great Recession of 2008. The recession then killed the jobs market, which left millions of former students unable to repay their loans. Thus, deregulation in general and the deregulation of the banking and finance industry in particular were primary drivers of the student loan crisis.

The loss of jobs pushed many students into default, but a student loan default did not have to lead to the many hardships that resulted: a loss of credit, ever-increasing loan balances, and an unwanted but unending relationship with bill collectors. Bankruptcy is supposed to save hopeless debtors from these trials and tribulations. No single act in this entire drama was more damaging to students or more responsible for creating the student loan crisis than the loss of bankruptcy protection for student loans.

For government to pass laws that give economic advantage to one group of citizens over another is to distort the very foundation of the capitalist system, so those who cheer loudest for that system, conservative Republicans, should be among the first to oppose those laws. Yet, in the case of discharging student loans through bankruptcy, the opposite was the case. In 1998 when bankruptcy protection was taken away on federal loans, and again in 2005 when it was removed from private bank loans, both houses of Congress were under Republican control and were being led by prominent conservative cheerleaders for the free market system.

Democrats, nonetheless, share some of the blame. The largess of the bankers had descended on them as well, and many had bought into much of the conservative analysis. Bill Clinton, the Democrat who signed the legislation taking bankruptcy protection away from federal student loans, became especially close to Wall Street bankers and leaders in the upper echelon of the finance elite.

That conservative politicians from both parties caved so easily to the interests of the banking industry revealed their own self-serving practices and the undue financial influence the industry was able to exert over them. Student loans were not among Wall Street's biggest businesses, yet they still cashed in enough of their political chips to demand and get new laws biased in their favor. The cynical politicians who facilitated these new laws were more concerned with their own survival in office than the conservative platitudes they so breathlessly directed at any passing microphone.

Our enemies in the fight to resolve the student loan crisis are the same people who created it in the first place: conservative politicians and Wall Street bankers. Their partnership is ongoing. For example, in the first quarter of 2013, Sallie Mae, the bank making the most private student loans, spent more than $1.4 million lobbying members of Congress. That's one bank in only three months! Meanwhile, bankers continue to treat the victims of the student loan crisis only as a source of profit, and conservative politicians on both sides of the aisle continue to do their bidding.

The origins of the student loan crisis reveal a vast transformation of our country, reshaped now by the conservative takeover at the end of the 1970s. That transformation is visible all around us. We see it in the lives of working people who now have to struggle longer and harder but earn significantly less. They are newly burdened by stresses and strains unfamiliar to previous generations. Many fathers now work two jobs while most mothers also work outside the home (in 1950, roughly 26% of women 25-54 did; by 2013, it was up to about 66%).

Less time is available to care for children, cultivate interests, or simply have fun. Too many kids are raised in substandard daycare centers, suffering emotionally and adding a new expense to the family budget. Nobody's at home after school. Weekends are for shopping and chores instead of recreation. Parents and children drift apart. Added stress leads to mental health problems. Family and community cohesiveness is diminished. Gun violence is commonplace, and the jails are filled with nonviolent drug offenders. This is what the conservative transformation of our government and culture has done to the American way of life in the past several decades.

Yet this dramatic transformation of our society happened so gradually that few of us realized its significance. Like the frog sitting in a pot of slowly boiling water, we are only just beginning to wake up to the dangers that confront us. It's a different country. Face it: the American dream has died. Conservative economic policy carried it to its grave. Now we have to build a new dream.

Chapter 7: The Hidden Cause Of The Decline In State Revenue

There is one final piece of the student loan puzzle to briefly describe before getting to the actions necessary to fix it. Initial tuition increases at public colleges and universities were due to cutbacks in funding from state legislatures, which in turn were due to reductions in state tax revenue. Not yet described is a major event in 1978 that triggered those reductions in state tax revenue, an event that played a dramatic role in launching the 30-year period of conservative dominance (1978-2008) that followed.

In the late 1970s, the newly reorganized conservative movement used "Get government off our backs" to motivate two separate constituencies. When addressed to the business community, the message was a demand for the repeal of government regulations, particularly those that protected the environment, prevented discrimination, enforced product safety regulations, and required a minimum wage. When directed to the voting public, on the other hand, the slogan was used as a cry for tax reduction.

Emphasizing tax cuts in the late 1970s was a smart play by conservatives. Many Americans were then suffering the high inflation and high unemployment of the Carter years. They, like the business community, wanted lower taxes. By using their catchy slogan, conservatives were able to harness the public's desire for lower taxes to the business community's demand for less government regulation. It was all part of a larger strategy to roll back the liberal policies and projects that had dominated government for the previous fifty years.

In their public campaigns, conservatives packaged the slogan with grossly exaggerated claims about government mismanagement and abuse, welfare fraud, arrogant bureaucrats, and assertions that taxes paid by hard working people were being wasted. Their effort, which continues, undermined American confidence in government and supported the larger conservative agenda. False as these attacks on government may have been, so many conservative politicians and pundits paid them lip service that they still have a powerful impact today.

In 1978, as this newly aggressive conservative approach showed its first signs of success, an opportunity for a road test appeared in California. An initiative to reduce property taxes was placed on the ballot there by a group of conservative activists. The successful passage of that initiative, Proposition 13, gave the conservative movement its first major victory and set the stage for much of what followed.

Proposition 13 was put forward as property tax relief for struggling homeowners, and indeed it did deliver significantly lower residential property taxes. But the money used to wage this successful campaign came from business interests. Written into the measure were parallel reductions in commercial property tax that gave business owners two-thirds of the eventual savings. Touted as the beginning of a new conservative struggle to lower taxes, the win enabled Ronald Reagan to build momentum for his victorious presidential campaign two years later.

But Proposition 13 was also instrumental in the dramatic rise in college tuition that eventually led to the student loan crisis. While the vote on the proposition had nothing to do with college tuition, it had everything to do with defunding state government. Proposition 13 instantly deprived California of billions of dollars in tax revenue. In the years after 1978, the resulting deficits literally crippled the state. Public schools were only one example. California had ranked first in the nation for its student-teacher ratio. In the years after Proposition 13, it sank to 49th, followed only by Mississippi. Other public services suffered similarly drastic cuts.

The conservative success in California inspired fiscal hawks in other states. When conservatives won control of their state legislatures, they cut taxes sharply and applied the proverbial meat ax to their state budgets. Conservatives stand in basic opposition to public services, believing that people must take responsibility for their own problems, so their public efforts to reduce taxes masked a less public desire to cut services.

In California, conservative legislators first cut welfare, unemployment compensation, and other services that disproportionately affected the poor. Eventually, however, they had to turn to public school budgets and appropriations for higher education. Those cuts had wider and more visible impact. The shock to the University of California (UC), the largest public institution of higher education in the country, is an example what happened elsewhere.

From the late 1960s to the late 1970s, when Proposition 13 passed, in-state tuition at UC was roughly $2,000, adjusted for inflation by using 2011 dollars (in actual dollars at the time, it was a tiny fraction of that amount). Because of the reduced revenues that resulted from Proposition 13, California legislators throughout the 1980s were forced to gradually cut appropriations for UC. The university had no choice but to slowly raise tuition.

By 1990, tuition was slightly more than $3,000 (in 2011 dollars). But after 1990, with California sinking deeper into debt, legislators could no longer hold the line. In the following years, as UC suffered further cuts, tuition was increased to compensate. By 2011, in-state tuition at UC had skyrocketed to $11,000, which put the university out of reach for most students and destroyed its chartered purpose of providing access to higher education for all Californians.

As mentioned earlier, in 2012 Ohio State University received only 7% of its budget from the state, down from 25% in 1990, while at the University of Washington the state funded 31% of a student's education in 2013, down from 64% ten years earlier. These were not isolated cases. Also mentioned earlier was a study showing that state funding for public colleges and universities across the country had dropped by an average of 7.6% in 2012, the largest single-year drop in half a century. Since publicly supported institutions like these account for roughly 80% of the national college population, it should be clear how massive cuts in state tax revenue led directly to significantly higher tuition for everyone.

Another milestone was reached in 2011 when for the first time public institutions of higher education in the U.S. received more money from students paying tuition than from state and local government. This shift in cost from the state to the student underscored the resounding victory conservatives had achieved in their successful effort to redefine higher education in America.

You can now see all the pieces that fit together to reveal how conservative economic policy is responsible for the student loan crisis. The pain being suffered by its victims is the collateral damage of a war fought by conservatives to limit government regulation and undercut the idea of collective social responsibility. Their policies survive today and provide Wall Street with the tools being used to enrich the wealthy at the expense of the rest of us.

Chapter 8: Demands That Would Save The Pre-2010 Borrowers

What then do we want government and the banking industry to do? What demands can we make that would give victims of the student loan crisis manageable debt payments and sufficient credit to function within the larger economy?

Any such demands will require the transfer of vast financial resources from the banks and the federal government to the borrowers. These demands would have to include fundamental changes to interest rates, collection procedures, payment obligations, co-signing requirements, and bankruptcy. Despite their radical and far-reaching nature, these demands must be carried out legally and in a way that is as fair as possible to all concerned, including the banks.

Clearly, to win such sweeping reform we will need to organize enormous political power. How to achieve that power is the topic of the next chapter. In this one, let's ignore for the moment any considerations of political impracticality and focus instead on four simple demands that taken together would bring a final and just resolution to the victims of the student loan swindle.

Overall, the loans that concern us can be divided into two broad categories, federal and private. The federal loans can also be divided into two categories: the vast majority that were made before 2010 by banks with a federal guarantee of repayment, and a much smaller number made between 1998 and

2010 with dollars from the Treasury before the new repayment rules were instituted. The private loans, in the second broad category, were made by banks directly to students or their families with no involvement by the government.

The first of our four demands focuses on the federal student loans. The solution for the pre-2010 borrowers who still carry these loans, as well as the few who took loans directly from the Treasury, is painfully simple: allow them to set their monthly payments in the same way that those who receive federal loans after 2010 can set theirs, that is, instead of fixed monthly payments, allow the payments to be a function of the borrower's income.

The new federal loan repayment system made available to some students after 2010 is the model. Let's take a closer look at how it works because two of the changes made are essential for all borrowers in trouble. First, lack of income can be accounted for, and second, the absence of bankruptcy protection is overcome.

Clearly, borrowers cannot repay loans without good jobs, and if good jobs are not available, without the ability to discharge the loan through bankruptcy they can face the threat of permanent financial ruin. Under the "Pay As You Earn Repayment Plan," the best of the federal loan repayment plans offered after 2010, monthly loan payments are limited to 10% of the borrower's discretionary income.

Discretionary income is determined using the Federal poverty level, which varies according to family size. First, a calculation is made to establish

150% of the appropriate poverty level for the borrower's family size. That amount is then subtracted from the borrower's total income. What remains is the borrower's discretionary income. If the borrower's earnings are less than 150% of the poverty level, the subtraction will result in a zero, in which case no monthly payments are required. If the borrower earns more than 150% of the federal poverty level, the maximum monthly payment the borrower is required to make is 10% of the difference, regardless of the size of the original loan.

This formulation automatically leaves the borrower with enough money to pay for the essentials of life: food, shelter, clothing and health care. And because borrowers who maintain these payments are not in arrears or delinquent, even if they make no payments, they do not suffer the same credit discrimination as other borrowers who fall behind in their fixed payments. Nor do their loans increase because of late fees and penalties.

Most post-2010 borrowers who don't have steady well-paying jobs will never be able to repay the entire amount of their student loans using this formula. Without access to bankruptcy they would otherwise be in danger of those loans steadily growing because of late fees and penalties, and of ending up with a lifetime problem. Instead, this new federal plan provides a solution.

If borrowers faithfully maintain monthly repayments of 10% of their discretionary income, even if in some or many of those months their income falls below the threshold of 150% of the poverty level and no payment is made, all obligations on the loan will nevertheless cease to exist after twenty years. Any balance remaining on the student loan at that time is erased. If the borrower works in a public interest capacity (teacher, soldier, fireman, charity worker), instead of twenty years, the loan balance will be fully erased after ten years.

Many problems remain with this plan. Interest rates are still far too high. The new federal loan amounts are too low to pay for most colleges, and the number of available loans is far less than the number of students who need them. As a result, many if not most students will also need private bank loans, which have few controls, no bankruptcy protection, and still must be repaid in full and on a fixed and inflexible schedule.

This is our first demand: Apply income-based repayment at 10% of discretionary income to all federal loans, past, present and future, with a twenty-year limit, ten for public interest workers. This will save those with pre-2010 federal student loans from credit discrimination, allow them to repay their loans when employment permits but maintain their good credit status if it does not, and for those who have loans more than twenty years old, it will deliver debt forgiveness even in the absence of bankruptcy protection.

To make such a solution work, Congress would have to rescind the original federal guarantees to the banks that put up the cash for the loans, as well as accept potential losses on the direct loans the government made after 1998. The banks would be deprived of billions of dollars in receivables. They would fight to stop this any way they could, starting with a claim that the withdrawal of the federal guarantees constitutes what lawyers call, "a taking."

Under our system of law, government must not use its power to arbitrarily take things of value from citizens or companies. It has done so during times of war, but on rare occasions it has also done so during peacetime by invoking its authority to deal with pending or actual economic emergencies, and those emergencies have taken a variety of forms.

During the Great Depression in the 1930s, the federal government forcibly closed numerous banks. In 1952, it seized the entire steel industry. In 1971, the federal government mandated wage and price controls across the nation. In addition, the federal government and most state and local governments have taken private property under their powers of eminent domain. They do this to further the overall economy and the public good, compensating owners, whether they like it or not, under court supervision.

In the case of the pre-2010 federal student loans, the government can use its emergency powers to rescind the loan guarantees given to the banks on the grounds that the ongoing student loan crisis places the entire American economy in jeopardy, and having benefited so much from that crisis, the banks must now make a sacrifice to end it. This position is supported by the fact that government acted inappropriately when it created the student loan business for the banks in 1965.

The next objection will be that our demand is unduly confiscatory, that is, even if it makes sense to "take" resources from the banks, we want to take more than they deserve to lose. That argument might leave some feeling sympathy for the banks, or a little queasy about the vast amount of money involved, so, let's look again at how much profit the banking industry actually made from their student loan business.

We saw in Chapter 5 that the Congressional Budget Office (CBO) expects total federal profits on student loans over the ten years between 2013 and 2023 to be $184 billion. That amount can be used to measure banking industry profit on federal loans in past decades. Prior to the 2008 recession, the spread between what the banks had to pay to get the money they lent (the Fed's discount rate) and the interest rate they charged student borrowers was comparable to the spread used by the CBO to estimate future profits.

While this is at best an approximation, it is likely that the banks made something close to $184 billion in the ten years before 2010, and a similar but diminishing amount in each of the two decades before that. Add to those hundreds of billions the tens to hundreds of billions more the banks made in windfall profits in 2009 and 2010, when they got a near-zero discount rate but continued to collect pre-recession interest rates from their federal student loan clients.

More profit was made from the 120% settlements given to the banks by the federal government to compensate for claims on defaulted loans. As we have seen, some of these claims were legitimate, while in the case of Sallie Mae and other big banks some were not. The banks realized a profit of 20% on each such claim, a gain for the bank on top of previous interest, late fees, and penalties paid.

Thus, without yet including profits the banking industry made on its private loans, and recognizing that back-of-the-envelop calculations like these are inherently dangerous, it nevertheless seems logical to conclude that the banks made somewhere in the neighborhood of one half a trillion dollars from their federal student loans business.

The bottom line is clear. With so much ill-gotten gain, ill gotten because it was facilitated by illegitimate government action, the banks can afford to take whatever losses they might now have to suffer on the federal loans they made.

As part of our first demand, we should also insist that borrowers with outstanding balances on federal loans be permitted to make their monthly payments to the federal government instead of the banks that put up the money. The federal government could then fix their monthly payments using the same formula it uses to determine payments for post-2010 borrowers who use the Pay As You Earn Repayment Plan, and then pass those monthly payments on to the appropriate bank.

If the government met our first demand, the banks would go to court to challenge its decision. Using methods outlined in the next chapter, we may be able to organize sufficient political power to prevent them from doing that. If we cannot, and if the courts decided in favor of the banks, some might argue that the borrowers could still receive the intended benefit of income-based repayment if the government meets its responsibilities under the guarantees and compensates the banks for whatever losses they incur under the new repayment plan.

Compensation like that would be grossly unfair to taxpayers. It would cost the government billions. There is no reason for taxpayers, among whom would be many of the 37 million pre-2010 federal borrowers, to lay out billions to compensate banks for their losses when collectively those same banks have already made far more billions on other loans.

Neither would it be fair for the government to utilize the one source of funds it could logically use to compensate the banks, namely, the profit it has already made on past federal student loans and the $184 billion it anticipates earning on new student loans between 2013 and 2023. That approach still requires that money be taken out of the Treasury and given to the banks. Such an act would merely transfer the injustice from the students to the taxpayers. There is only one fair resolution: make the banks take the loss.

That approach can be applied with equal logical to the second broad category of student loans, the bank loans that did not come with a federal guarantee but were private transactions between the bank and the borrower. On the surface, these private bank loans present a more complex problem because they involve contracts that are purely commercial transactions between non-governmental entities.

Nevertheless, justice demands that outstanding balances on these private transactions be treated exactly the same as the federal loans: limit repayment obligations to 10% of discretionary income and forgive any remaining balance after twenty years. There is a difference between the two types of loans, the federal and the private, but when the banks convinced the federal government to remove bankruptcy protection from private loans in 2005, they lost the right to any claim of unfair treatment they might otherwise make now. So much unearned profit was derived from this blatant government misconduct that fairness demands a severe penalty.

Furthermore, after the economic crash in 2008, the banks also realized windfall profits on their private student loans. Those profits came when, as part of the economic recovery, the Fed lowered the discount rate charged to the banks, first to 0.50% and then to 0.75%. This was done with no requirement that the banks pass these taxpayer-sponsored benefits on to their student loan clients. It was a windfall because the banks continued to charge pre-recession interest rates, often as much as 8.5%, on their private student loans.

This outrageous greed becomes even harder to stomach because these "too big to fail" banks were at the same time receiving massive federal bailouts. The banks made huge and unconscionable profits on the backs of students at the same time that they were gratefully accepting federal welfare in the form of bailouts and artificially low interest rates.

This is our second demand: force the banks to accept income-based repayment for all of their private student loans, before and after 2005. This would be fair compensation for their exorbitant profits while simultaneously providing a just solution for the borrowers. Again, government has emergency powers with which to make the banks comply.

A long list of misdeeds justifies such an extreme solution. Government, which should have protected the public interest, instead empowered and enriched a private entity. It approved discriminatory legislation that arbitrarily removed bankruptcy protection from legal student loans. It permitted the banks to charge interest rates only slightly below market instead of demanding much lower rates for students. It removed a host of consumer protections from student loans, like truth-in-lending provisions and regulations limiting the behavior of unscrupulous bill collectors.

We estimated the massive profits captured by the banks on federally guaranteed student loans. Their profits on the private bank loans are more difficult to assess but are likely to be almost as high. There were fewer private loans, but the interest and fees on them were much higher than those permitted on the federal loans. The banks also engaged in more vigorous collection practices for the private loans since they did not come with federal guarantees. Thus, it is possible that the banking industry's collective profits from private student loans approached what they made on their federal loans.

While it is a very rough but a relatively conservative approximation, the evidence presented in Chapter 5 suggested that since the beginning of the student loan program the banking industry may have funneled a total of somewhere between $500 and $800 billion out of the pockets of college students and their families and on to their own balance sheets. The bulk of this transfer would have occurred in more recent years when the need for student loans was greatest. It would be simple justice, however irregularly achieved, to use the government to force the banks to give some of that money back.

Emergency legislation could define past banking practices with respect to student loans as having been in violation of various fair trade regulations. With such a finding, the government could then define a remedy. Two possibilities exist. The government can assume collection of these private loans under the same system as the federal loans, forwarding whatever payments are made to the banks that provided the loans. Or, the government can simply force the banks to limit their collections to a criterion of 10% of disposable income and forgive any loans more than twenty years old. If the second, far less preferable, option is chosen, past practice indicates that harsh penalties will be needed to effectively discipline the banks.

The third of our four demands applies to the interest rates on all student loans, federal and private, past, present and future. Our first two demands will make monthly payments affordable for all borrowers, federal and private, and even in the absence of bankruptcy protection, will relieve them of debt after twenty years. Nonetheless, the interest rates on these loans remain far too high. Thanks to income-based repayment, borrowers will not have bigger monthly payments than they can afford, but many will still have to pay much more than they should.

High interest rates enlarge the amount borrowers owe, even if late fees and penalties are not charged. That actually discriminates against those borrowers capable of paying off their loans. The higher interest rates and the resulting larger principal will mean that for these borrowers the period of their indebtedness will be unfairly extended. Since the government failed to adequately control interest rates from the beginning, the best solution now would be to not only lower them, but reduce them to non-profit levels.

America once embraced the idea that government has a responsibility to prepare young people for productive lives, that giving youth the training needed to meaningfully contribute to our overall economy benefits us all. That was the fundamental idea behind public schools and our tradition of public education. That tradition grew because our forebears realized that a minimum level of citizen education was necessary both for a well functioning democracy and a healthy economy. We would be outraged if government charged tuition in our public schools. Is it any more outrageous for a private bank or the federal government to charge interest rates on student loans that then lead to unconscionable profits – or any profit at all?

Economic survival for young people, as well as their ability to contribute to a well functioning economy, now requires more than a grade school and high school education. If government had a responsibility to facilitate primary and secondary education in the past, that responsibility should include higher education in the future.

In the long run, the United States has to find a way to return to a system of public universities funded primarily by government in which a large majority of our young people can get the education they need without having to borrow money. In the short run, since access to higher education continues to require inordinately large loans, we can at least be sure that those loans are issued to students on a non-profit basis.

A compelling argument can be made that financing higher education, any education past secondary school, contributes to America's economic and national security. If that argument is valid, government has a responsibility to subsidize all or part of the cost. If banks participate, as they have been since the student loan program began in 1965, they should be forced to do so on a strictly non-profit basis.

The banking industry has an obligation to contribute to our economic and national security by offering such non-profit rates to students and their families. Public service of this nature should be part of the trade-off by which government sanctions the banks and allows them to operate, much as the federal government requires television stations to make public service announcements in exchange for their use of the electromagnetic spectrum. Given the critical role the banking industry plays in our economy, it should be regulated in the same way as a public utility or a defense contractor forced to work on a cost-plus basis.

A description of the interest rates that Congress has mandated for future federal student loans was presented in Chapter 5. To summarize, these rates will equal the varying ten-year Treasury bond rate plus 2.05% for college students and 3.60% for graduate students. Those small bumps of 2.05% and 3.60% are far from trivial. In fact, they are huge. They are the main reason why the CBO projects profits of $184 billion for federal student loans between 2013 and 2023.

While the debate about the interest on future federal loans is not directly relevant to a discussion of what interest rate would be fair for the past loans, the issues involved do relate to the past loans and will help explain why a non-profit rate is the best solution.

As previously described, the federal government regularly borrows money by selling Treasury bonds. These bonds are in effect a loan for which the government pays a fixed interest rate over a fixed period. While Congress debated proper interest rates for federal student loans in 2013, loans that are considered to be for a ten-year period, the government was selling ten-year Treasury bonds with an interest rate that fluctuated between 2% and 3%.

The massive government profit that will be generated by the new interest rate formula based on these Treasury bonds is the opposite of good government policy. It functions as an additional tax on students and their families, limits the potential of working class and poor students to advance, and creates a population of defaulting borrowers who will be a brake on the overall economy. Government's role is to facilitate the education of young people, not as an act of charity as conservatives would have it, but because doing so protects democratic institutions, expands the economy, and adds to the common good.

Until our government can be made to fund higher education itself, as so many other industrialized countries do, it can still help young people get an education by providing non-profit interest rates on their educational loans. Those interest rates can most easily be determined by making the student loan rate equal to the Federal Reserve's discount rate.

Prior to the 2008 recession, the discount rate was in the 5% to 6% range. After it, the Fed lowered the discount rate to near zero to stimulate the economy and to save the banks that were judged, "too big to fail." In 2009, the discount rate was 0.50%. The next year, it was raised to 0.75%, and as of the beginning of 2014, it has remained there.

If a bank can acquire money from the Federal Reserve at this low rate, why can't a college student? Isn't the logic that claims a multi-billion dollar bank is too *big* to fail weaker than the logic that argues a working class college kid is too *small* to fail? How does it make sense for past student borrowers to continue paying interest rates as high as 6.8% on their federal loans and even higher interest rates on their bank loans, when the banks get the money they lend for only 0.75%?

Earlier it was mentioned that Senator Elizabeth Warren had tried unsuccessfully to introduce legislation to lower the federal student loan interest rate to the Fed's discount rate. Her bill failed to get out of committee, even though it only addressed interest rates on *future* federal student loans. This is yet another indication of how difficult it will be to bring real relief to the victims of the student loan crisis and why that relief can only be achieved outside the usual legal and legislative channels.

This is our third demand: immediately reduce all interest rates on all outstanding student loans, federal and private, to the Federal Reserve's discount rate, and fix that rate for the life of the loan. Anything less than this, any rate that would be higher, would allow the banks and the government to continue making outrageous profits on the backs of students and families they have already abused. Taxpayers bailed out the banks. Now it's time for the banks to bail out the students they so egregiously exploited.

To force interest rates down retroactively also requires the emergency powers of government, since these rates were set in the original loan contracts. However, the same rationale for using those powers in pursuit of our other two demands applies equally to the setting of interest rates.

Our final demand is for the return of bankruptcy protection and consumer loan regulations for all student loans, past and future. Bankruptcy protection is not necessary for loans that will be forgiven after twenty years (ten, in the case of public interest workers) because income-based payment schedules mean the borrowers will not be impoverished by fixed monthly payments, and they will be out from under all debt at the end of that period. Nonetheless, along with the other consumer protections, bankruptcy must be restored.

This is our fourth demand: repeal the laws that removed bankruptcy protection from federal student loans in 1998 and private bank loans in 2005, and reinstate all consumer protections removed from educational loans. Passing these laws and repealing these protections were acts of official discrimination. They must be repudiated. Future student borrowers may some day become subject to new repayment arrangements that make bankruptcy and other consumer protections critical once again.

Few borrowers who have income-based payments will benefit directly from a return of bankruptcy protection, but all will be helped by reinstating the other consumer protections taken away during the same period. Those few who might be helped by bankruptcy protection may need a "fresh start" free of all debt to obtain certain kinds of credit. Other borrowers, however, will still need truth-in-lending disclosures, safeguards against undue garnishments, defenses against unscrupulous bill collectors, and the full range of consumer loan protections.

No one wants to see any more grandmothers lose a portion of their social security checks because they generously co-signed a student loan for a grandchild. Nor should there be co-signing parents who lose their homes and have to live with relatives, or even the child for whom the original loan was co-signed, because their own income is insufficient to both make the loan payments and live decently. The best way to be certain outrages like this never happen again is to reinstate bankruptcy protection and all consumer loan protections on all legal loans, educational or otherwise.

Here then are the four simple demands that can rescue the victims of the student loan swindle:

1) Apply income-based repayment at 10% of discretionary income to all federal loans, past, present and future, with a twenty-year limit, ten for public interest workers.

2) Force the banks to accept the same income-based repayment plan for all of their private student loans, before and after 2005.

3) Immediately reduce all interest rates on all outstanding student loans, federal and private, to the Federal Reserve's discount rate, and fix that rate for the life of the loan.

4) Repeal the laws that removed bankruptcy protection from federal student loans in 1998 and private bank loans in 2005, and reinstate all consumer protections removed from educational loans.

The next step is to organize a massive public pressure campaign. If we succeed, we can then build enough political power to force these four demands on the federal government and the banking industry. We start weak and unorganized, while our opponents have enormous power, limitless resources, and at present no reason to compromise. It sounds daunting, but there is a way to do it.

Chapter 9: Organizing The Political Power Needed To Win

Time to storm the castle. If you are a victim of the student loan crisis, you now know its history, its size and scope, how it started and grew, who made it happen, and what needs to be done to fix it. You also know that the desperate situation you are in did not happen by accident. It was caused by Wall Street titans, conservative ideologues, and groveling politicians. They don't deserve your respect, only your anger and outrage. They have taken from you something very precious, a chance for a secure financial future, and as you work to take it back, you will need to be both creative and doggedly determined.

You now have four demands that would correct the abuse and injustice created by the student loan system. There is little doubt that Congress and the President have the power to grant these demands, given what they have done in the face of past emergencies. Many will disagree. Ignore them. Your job is to build the political power necessary to win these demands, not argue about the technical or legal complications involved in the fight. Let your lawyers debate their lawyers. You need to focus on winning political power…because anything can happen once you have enough of it.

It is folly to think that government will approve these reforms simply on the basis of fundamental fairness. The banking industry, through its massive financial support of politicians, exerts much more influence over Congress than you do. Our government's recent history indicates a belief that some banks are "too big to fail" and must be protected even if the financial interests of the rest of us are sacrificed. Conventional wisdom will argue that we are isolated and alone and our prospects nonexistent.

But we don't have to be isolated and alone. If you are a victim of these student loan swindles, you are one of millions. Conventional wisdom can be turned on its head if enough borrowers join together and embrace a strategy that begins with two challenges – challenges likely to push you out of your comfort zone, but challenges that millions of others in almost every successful social movement in history have been required to meet: you must organize yourselves into a disciplined and cohesive movement, and you must be prepared to break the law.

Nonviolent movements that succeed in transforming society almost always involve widespread nonviolent law breaking, and while some individuals in these movements are made to suffer as a result, the vast majority escape any consequences, either because of the eventual success of the movement or because there were simply too many people to punish.

In the early 20th Century, women often violated laws banning demonstrations and marches to win the right to vote. Later, factory workers violated property laws by seizing manufacturing plants and outlasting legally sanctioned strikebreakers to win the right to organize labor unions. In the South, black and white activists broke laws on a massive scale to build the modern civil rights movement. So did the antiwar protestors of the 1960s, and all the movements since that have so profoundly reshaped our society. Absent a willingness to break the law, to engage in nonviolent civil disobedience, achievements like these can rarely be won.

How can similar tactics be applied to win relief for victims of the student loan crisis? By striking, by refusing to make any more payments until the four demands are met, not as individuals, one person at a time, but on a huge scale in which millions refuse simultaneously, and, as a result, swamp the ability of the government and the banks to effectively counter them.

In the opening chapter, I described the classic rent strike in which tenants withhold rent from a negligent landlord until the landlord's ongoing expenses (utilities, property tax, mortgage payments, maintenance), and simultaneous lack of incoming payments, force a settlement. If enough people join such a struggle and remain committed, their staying power will determine the outcome. Even slum tenants, among the least powerful people in our society, have gone up against well-connected landlords, violated their leases by withholding rent, resisted threats of arrest, lawsuits and evictions, and, if they held out long enough, eventually won. That is the model upon which to base our strategy.

There are two advantages in using this model, benefits that can lead to enough political power to win. First, with 37 million Americans still paying off pre-2010 federal loans, and millions more similarly indebted to private banks, we have the opportunity to organize not just hundreds of thousands of collaborators but millions, many millions. Second, the explosive advance of the Internet and online social media give us the tools needed to quickly and cheaply reach out to those millions, explain our purposes, and inspire their participation.

The government and the banks are more vulnerable to a tactic like this than either would admit. Punishments for wrongdoing in our society are designed to control the behavior of individuals. But when massive numbers of people commit such acts simultaneously and together, as they do in nonviolent civil disobedience campaigns, the responses available to the government and the courts are less effective. Governmental authority can rapidly collapse if large numbers of people collectively defy it by breaking a law, the more so if they remain unified. In such cases, the ability to punish nonviolent resistors (absent machine guns) often evaporates.

The government and the banks that made federal and private student loans each have a cash flow to manage, just like landlords. They receive money from borrowers and use that money to pay their own ongoing expenses. In the case of the government, those expenses include benefit checks for Social Security and Medicare recipients, salaries for government employees, bills due for government purchases, and the myriad other payments the government is obligated to make every day.

Since the government has vast resources at its disposal, cash flow is more critical for a bank, whether it is a stand-alone or a giant like the Bank of America. For these private banks, ongoing expenses have to be covered by monthly income. Their wealth is tied up in investments. That's why they are in business. That wealth is not readily available to pay bills. Their ongoing need for monthly income creates a massive vulnerability.

So, we start weak compared to the banking industry and the government. But they have weaknesses as well, weaknesses that can be exploited by the power we can organize. First, we have the power to cut off money they urgently need. Second, we have the power to prevent them from punishing us. These powers come with overwhelming numbers, and both can be ours if we recruit a sufficient number of determined participants.

Our strategy, therefore, has to be based on the recruitment of those participants. That begins with a website. The website would contain educational materials about the student loan crisis and the demands we are making for its resolution, but it's primary function would be to organize victims of the crisis into a strike force. They would be asked to sign a statement pledging to withhold all student loan repayments if and when the total of others who make the same pledge reaches some pre-selected but very large number, say, five million.

Is there a realistic hope that such a large number can be reached? Evidence indicates there is. There are six million borrowers already in default on federal student loans and an unknown number in default on private bank loans. They are not part of our target audience because they have already stopped making loan repayments. However, there are as many as twelve million borrowers with federal loans who are delinquent, meaning that they are still trying to make payments but are chronically behind. Similarly, there are an unknown number delinquent on private bank loans.

All borrowers currently delinquent have good reason to consider making the pledge, but so do millions of others not yet delinquent but in a constant struggle to keep up with their payments. The sign-ups may build slowly but as the number of pledges mount and the effort becomes more visible, more of these borrowers will become curious, investigate what is happening, and find the courage to join. Five million, given the stakes and given the misery experienced by these people, seems achievable.

At first glance, it appears that participation would be risky, that borrowers will fear reprisals from the authorities. But those reprisals are a myth. There is no legal jeopardy attached to signing a pledge. Those pledging would continue to pay down their loans, just as they do now. People cannot be arrested, sued, penalized or given a lower credit rating for a pledge to take some future action as long as there is no change in their present behavior. So, actually, the pledge itself would not require much courage. The only danger comes when the threshold number of pledges, five million in this example, is reached and each individual has to act.

There is more to say about that danger, but first let's imagine the proposed website. There would be a place for borrowers to sign the pledge. Each would be asked to name the individual bank or banks to which they owe money, whether it is for a federal loan or a private loan. Individual graphs or thermometers on the website would show the rising number of total pledges, as well as the number of payment strikers prepared to defy each individual bank.

Consider what would happen as these numbers mount and become politically significant. A potential payment strike in which first thousands and then millions plan to simultaneously refuse their legal obligations would be one of the most compelling news stories of the day. The media would closely monitor progress toward the target of five million. Pundits would fill the airwaves with a raging debate about the morality of the action. The banks would issue repeated denunciations. The government would threaten the participants. Opponents would spin lurid yarns about the ulterior motives of the leaders.

And, of course, publicity like that would play right into our hands. The story would engage the nation, and the widespread news coverage would inspire more victims of the student loan swindle to join the effort. Meanwhile, many Americans not personally affected would identify with the protesting former students. Many would see the fight as a David vs. Goliath struggle and take the side of the little guy. Once such a public battle is joined and receives widespread news coverage, other forces would join the fight.

Conservative ideologues, Wall Street financiers, right wing Republicans, and most corporate and business leaders would decry the effort. But labor unions, advocacy groups, consumer organizations, and progressives would support it. They would see a unique opportunity to expose the damage conservatives have done to America. The fact that so many borrowers, who collectively represent a broad spectrum of political opinion, have overcome their differences and united in their own self-interest behind a militant and radical action would be seen as an added bonus. A national political firestorm would result.

Note that all this will happen before anyone who has made a pledge is required to act on it. Unlike a rent strike, which begins with the actual withholding of rent, a payment strike like this only requires a pledge, so it is far easier to join. The power of this strategy comes in part from the fact that there is no risk associated with making a pledge but enormous risk to the banks and the government as the number of pledges increases. Once this is realized by the tens of millions of borrowers, some will rush to the website to sign up. Then, as the number of pledges mounts and our opponents begin to understand the enormity of what might be coming, panicked bankers will appeal to Congress for relief.

That is exactly what we want them to do. Of course, Congress initially will help the bankers. But Congress is the one institution of government most vulnerable to public opinion, and the court of public opinion is the one place we can most easily prevail. Therefore, Congress is the most favorable terrain upon which to mount this fight. Under normal circumstances, public opinion exerts only minimal control over congressional decision-making because government and the mass media constantly manipulate public opinion to support a pro-business political agenda. Yet, there are times when public opinion can arise spontaneously, escape that manipulation, and overwhelm Congress.

It is only in such moments that genuine transformations take place. Our agenda must be to first prevail in the court of public opinion and then use our victory there to overwhelm Congress. Only then can our demands be given the force of law, and only the force of law will be sufficient to overcome the power of the banking industry.

While a small minority in Congress will be sympathetic, the vast majority will greet us with overwhelming hostility. They will resist, threaten, cajole, and offer toothless compromises, but they will not seriously consider our demands. We have to be equally obstinate. We will only get what we want through the application of brute force. Congress, as an institution, is not our friend. Congress first passed the laws that exploited those who accepted the old federal student loans, and it is Congress that now exploits those who accept the new ones by demanding interest rates that lead to exorbitant profits for the government.

Both political parties played a role in this. Republicans going back before the Reagan era embraced the conservative ideology that first caused and then justified the student loan abuses. Much later,

President George W. Bush, the Republican conservative-in-chief, embraced the worst of those abuses when he signed the 2005 law removing bankruptcy protection from private student loans.

Democrats were only marginally better. Often ambivalent or split on the critical issues, they took too much money from Wall Street and the banking sector to be able to stand up to them and protect the interests of students. It was a Democrat, Bill Clinton, who signed the bill ending bankruptcy protection for federal student loans in 1998. Democrats will support our goals long before Republicans, but not until we force them to do so.

As the number of pledges grows, Congress will watch nervously. Members will wonder how high the total will go, what the staying power of those who sign the pledge will be, and whether or not they will actually follow through on what they have promised. Controversy will swirl around the issue and the participants, and constant attempts will be made to assess our strengths and weaknesses. In the midst of this turmoil, there will be actions we can take to keep the controversy alive and increase the fear bubbling up among government officials and banking executives.

For example, as pledges pour in, the lists of borrowers who owe money to specific banks will build to large numbers. Those individual banks can then be targeted for organized protest. If the website comes to have hundreds of thousands who owe money to the Bank of America, as one example, they can all be asked to picket branches of the bank across the country, all on the same day, or on the first day of every month. A protest like that would garner national press coverage, embarrassing the bank and driving away some of its customers.

Similarly, all those who owe money to Sallie Mae could be organized over a single day or a single week to shut down their online and telephone operations by flooding them with legitimate requests. All such actions are legal protests and involve no real jeopardy for those who participate. But interim actions of this sort would go a long way toward fortifying the resolve of those who signed the pledge, and convincing those who signed only as a protest to be ready to actually strike. Opponents will complain that tactics like this border on blackmail. They are correct. This is about force, not persuasion.

Another possible action, which would put pressure on the federal government and its judicial system, involves the bankruptcy courts. Under the laws that took away bankruptcy protection for student loans, a provision was left in place that allows borrowers to file for bankruptcy if they can demonstrate extreme hardship. The claimed extreme hardship, however, must be validated in a court hearing, and in practice the courts have regularly denied this status to student loan borrowers. Nonetheless, if a request for an extreme hardship exception is made, the court must set a hearing. That's a vulnerability that can also be exploited.

Hundreds of thousands of borrowers who had made a pledge to withhold payments and who each had a need for "a fresh start" could all simultaneously file for a bankruptcy hearing on the basis of extreme hardship. Our website could provide the borrowers with instructions about how to do that and even give them copies of all the paperwork required. No lawyers would be necessary.

The federal bankruptcy courts would be overwhelmed and unable to function. If they reverted to blanket denials, the borrowers could shift to filing countering lawsuits that would further paralyze the court system, again with legal papers provided by the website. Teams of volunteer lawyers could easily be recruited in advance to file more formal and complex lawsuits in order to block or delay any legislative attempts to alter the extreme hardship procedure.

Protests and mass actions like these can be combined with periodic newsletters and emails customized to various groups among those signing the pledge. Damning information about specific banks, news about legal struggles between banks and individual borrowers, proposed legislation for or against the strikers, attacks on them made by bankers and conservatives, all can be used to maintain the motivation of those who have pledged.

The website would become a dynamic center of activism, protest, information and concentrated outrage. The public and the news media would be encouraged to visit. Outreach to those who had made the pledge would be frequent and interesting. The four demands around which all the action and information are organized would be trumpeted at every opportunity. Open debates would be conducted with opponents so the underlying issues are publicly exposed. And above all, a constant attempt would be made to provide the news media with emotional and provocative stories about individual victims so the David vs. Goliath aspect of the struggle would remain prominent and engaging – and add to the pressure on Congress.

Do not underestimate the possibility that congressional resistance to our demands will collapse before the pledges actually have to be honored. That would be the best outcome for the borrowers, but clear heads on the other side might see that it is also the best outcome for the government and the banks. If the time comes, in our example, when four million borrowers have made the pledge and the total is rapidly building toward the five million threshold that would trigger the payment strike, with the news media focusing national attention on the coming showdown, pressure on Congress to resolve the conflict would be extreme.

For that pressure to be effective, all concerned must be convinced that the majority of those pledging will actually follow through. If the banking industry believes that millions who owe it money are poised to openly repudiate their debts, they will think twice about continuing to stand firm, not just because of the money they could lose but because a payment strike would be a public relations disaster for them. People are already hostile toward bankers; some now refer to the Wall Street variety as "banksters." Given how sensitive the banking industry is to regulations imposed by Congress, they can ill afford a further decline in their public stature.

Any individual bank seen as forcing potential strikers to act on their pledges is a bank likely to be boycotted by many of their supporters. Banks make hard financial calculations. Their owners and managers will realize that if a strike goes forward, it might cost them profits they are currently well positioned to realize. They will understand that they already have vast capital, favorably laws, a pliable political system, and a corporate culture in which they exert inordinate influence. Conceding to the demands of the payment strikers would cost them billions, but some among of them are likely to think that those billions may be worth forfeiting in order to protect even more billions they can make going forward.

The government, too, will want to avoid a payment strike and is likely to go to extremes to prevent one. Governments fear disorder. When events get out of control in one arena, disorder often spreads to others. Our government and the powers that support and depend on it do not want to see a mass movement gain power and influence by acting in defiance of its authority. Many officials now understand that when government threatens to punish a large number of people and those people ignore the threat and willing accept the punishment, that officials look toothless and government has limited its other options.

That is what happened during the civil rights movement in the South. Segregationist state and local governments threatened people with jail if they did not stop protesting discriminatory Jim Crow laws. Most of the protestors felt that a jail term and a criminal record was a price worth paying for an opportunity to oppose racial discrimination. They advocated a strategy to "fill up the jails," which left authorities with little room to house other prisoners, a clogged court calendar, greater expense, and nothing else with which to threaten the protestors.

That strategy inspired a culture of protest in the South that led many more people to join the effort. With no credible threat left to them, state and local governmental authority either collapsed in the face of protestor demands or reverted to overt violence. In either case, popular support for the movement grew. It was a lesson in civil disobedience that few on either side of those battles ever forgot.

It is for these reasons that Congress and the banking industry might grant our demands before payments have to be withheld, and before anyone is exposed to legal repercussions. In the face of millions of borrowers standing firm and being ready to repudiate their loan agreements, cooler heads in government and the banking industry may realize that in the long run they have more to gain by giving in than by instituting legal proceedings against people with limited resources, proceedings likely to cost them more than they will ever recover.

However, a positive outcome like that is clearly dependent upon the determination of those who make the pledges. If that determination dissipates and divisions appear among them, there is little likelihood that our opponents will settle without an actual strike. Victory will not come unless our opponents believe that those who made the pledges have the capacity to follow through on their threats and remain united.

No one can predict how the banking industry will respond, or if individual banks within the industry will all go along with a collective approach. Similarly, no one knows whether Congress's desire for stability and predictability will motivate it to defend the industry at all costs, or, as it was forced to do during the Great Depression, throw the banks under the bus to preserve the larger economic order. It is in the midst of such crises that Congress can be most responsive to public demands, and as the history of the Great Depression indicates, most open to radical transformation.

Nonetheless, despite the potential for chaos, boycotts and lost profits, a misguided banking industry may be powerful enough to block a congressional solution before the pledges have to be acted upon. What happens then? What options will the government and the bankers have if on a single day most of the five million borrowers who had signed pledges announce that they have stopped repaying their student loans?

At the start, the story will dominate the news and reverberate across the country, but the fiscal impact on the banking industry would not be immediately crippling. However, as the weeks go by, if various threats leveled against the payment strikers by banking and government officials are ignored and the strike continues, the balance of forces will gradually shift. When the weeks turn into months, and the banks begin to suffer more massive losses, their cash flow will come under increasing and significant pressure.

At the same time, if legal sanctions are filed against the strikers and/or legal collections activity begun against them, the nation's prosecutors, judges, and law enforcement personnel will quickly understand that they lack the resources to go after very many of them. Disciplining even a small portion of the strikers would be a gargantuan task that would leave the legal system unable to fulfill its other responsibilities. Even if law enforcement officials at the top decide to go after the payment strikers, some closer to the ground will question and resist that decision – and more than a few will owe money on student loans themselves.

Victory in a battle like this depends upon the determination of the strikers. It's a game of chicken. If the strikers hold out long enough, and legal action cannot stop them because they are prepared to ignore the threats, the banks will have no choice but to give in. Similarly, if the government is incapable, as they are, of taking simultaneous legal action against millions of strikers, and if its threats also play to deaf ears, Congress too would have no choice but to capitulate.

However, before either the banks or the government give in, they will throw up a fog of proposed compromises and alternatives. These compromises will test the organizing and educational work done while the pledges were being collected. Strikers have to anticipate false and misleading compromises and build their resistance against them.

Any break in their unity will defeat them. This must be clear from the beginning. Whatever resources are required to carry out this inoculation must be part of the plan. Unity is a critical factor. If the unity of the strikers is maintained, it is difficult to see what anyone or anything could do to stop them.

Significant harm might come to a portion of the strikers once payments are withheld. Government or banking officials will make an example of a few to break the unity of the many. This could include a loss of credit rating, wage garnishment, lawsuits, other financial harassment, or actual criminal charges for offenses like conspiracy. This is serious stuff. Even a hit on one's credit rating can make it impossible to rent an apartment or secure a car loan. And, of course, criminal charges can lead to jail time. Despite the fact that these harms are less than what people have had to face in other struggles, the banks and the government can direct punishing blows against at least a few of the strikers.

To succeed, solidarity must be maintained no matter how severe the threats. The risks strikers face are real and must be weighed against the rewards they seek and the outrage they feel. In struggles like this the authorities always single out a few individuals in order to intimidate the others. But in this case, the resources available to the authorities are limited. All the prosecutors, judges, process servers and collection agencies in the country couldn't begin to take on five million additional cases.

If intimidating actions are attempted against some of the strikers, the odds of any one individual suffering negative consequences are diminishingly small. Even if 5,000 strikers are targeted, a massive undertaking, the odds of any one individual out of five million being affected are only a thousand to one. Even if 50,000 actions are filed, a far more immense task, the odds are only a hundred to one.

Certainly, some will be hurt, and each person participating has to be ready to be among them. It's like going to a political demonstration. Most are completely safe, but once in a while arrests are made and physical fights break out. Those who participate have to be ready either way. In general, protestors go to these events not because it is safe to do so but because they believe the risk of harm is small.

Maintaining solidarity after the payment strike begins is the only way to win. If a victory is achieved, any legal sanctions, lawsuits or punishments aimed at individual strikers can easily be undone. Successful strikers will be able to demand that prosecutors drop all legal charges, banks withdraw all lawsuits, and collection agencies reverse all penalties. Punishment-reversing actions like these are part of the settlement in any successful strike. The fact is, if we have enough political power to win our four demands, we will have more than enough to undo any harm that government or banking authorities caused any of the strikers.

****

The struggle envisioned here could be a turning point for America. The example of victims of the student loan crisis standing up for themselves and successfully facing down the federal government and the banking industry could inspire others to similar action. Our government is gridlocked and for the foreseeable future is unlikely to change. This is a time when citizen action can fill the void and transform the country.

The example of an organized and powerful movement put together by people who lack financial resources may be just what we need to address America's other underlying problems, like severe income inequality and unconscionable poverty. The era of conservative dominance is ending, giving us new opportunities to rebuild the America they have left in ruins.

The student loan crisis will not be resolved in favor of the borrowers until the borrowers organize themselves and go outside the law. The conservative politicians responsible for the crisis and the bankers who have been enriched by it will not agree to a meaningful resolution until enough force has been applied to overcome their greed and self-interest.

Can a movement led by borrowers who lack the funds to repay their student loans actually achieve such a challenging goal? That depends upon how angry they get.

Fifty years ago, young black students with little more than a desire for justice sparked the civil rights movement. Later, during the war in Viet Nam, millions of people, young and old, opposed the foreign policy and military might of the most powerful nation on Earth. They protested, risked arrest, were injured by Billy clubs and fists, but maintained their unity and eventually prevailed. Since then, powerless Americans have launched powerful new movements to advocate for gays, women, farmworkers, ethnic groups, the disabled, immigrants, animal rights, environmental protection, and more.

The strategy I have advocated is an old strategy clothed in new technology. Half a century ago, I saw it work in the South when civil rights activists "filled up the jails" to block more arrests and clog the courts. I saw it again when hundreds or thousands of arrested antiwar demonstrators all demanded jury trials knowing that the courts lacked the capacity to grant them and had no alternative but to drop charges. Instead of retreating in the face of more powerful opposition, successful social movements like these found the cracks in their opponent's armor and developed the tactics necessary to exploit them.

Today, that task has been made far easier thanks to Internet communications and social media platforms. The power citizens have to refuse, to say "no," has always been a threat to those who rule or dominate them. But that threat only succeeds if a critical mass of people come together and act collectively. That is why the Internet is such a powerful new tool. For the first time, it allows the leaders and coordinators of mass movements to communicate with millions of potential supporters and sympathizers instantaneously and at virtually no cost. It's full potential has yet to be realized.

The federal government and the banking industry conspired to financially exploit college students and their families on a massive scale. The purpose of this book is to urge you to conspire back. Use the tools now at your disposal to raise a movement strong enough to right this wrong. Yes, it will require sacrifice, and determination, and time. But it can be done. All it takes is a few dedicated and far-seeing people willing to come together to provide the leadership. Perhaps you're one of them.

Appendix: What To Do In The Meantime

If you are a victim of the student loan crisis, I know the situation you are in is a difficult one, and I don't want to suggest that the strategy I have outlined in this book is the only action you can take. That strategy has drawbacks. It requires a great deal of organizational work and talent and a dogged determination that would have to last a long time. There are other actions available immediately that will not solve your fundamental problem but might provide some short-term relief or a modest improvement in your individual circumstances.

Some websites have already gathered large numbers of signatures on petitions to the government for various kinds of student loan relief. You should get involved with them. These websites are making the student loan crisis visible to large numbers of people and are building support for reform. Many in your situation who may not yet be ready for the militant strategy I am advocating should first participate in efforts like these. Perhaps later, out of building frustration, stronger action will become more appealing.

Meanwhile, these web-directed campaigns provide important vehicles to keep the pressure on government officials and to maintain the newsworthiness of and the public interest in the ongoing student loan crisis. When you are able, visit www.StudentDebtCrisis.org and www.IamNotaLoan.org, sign their petitions and get on their mailing lists.

Many struggling with student loans will also need immediate advice about how to stay out of default, hold off aggressive bill collectors, preserve credit ratings, prevent wage garnishment, and so forth. That advice has been compiled for you at www.StrikeDebt.org. There you can download, "The Debt Resistors' Operations Manual." The Manual provides numerous tips on how you can postpone payments. It also includes legal forms you can download, model letters, and other materials that could be very useful in your dealings with government officials, banks, and collection agencies.

Acknowledgements

Several people shared their expertise with me or were kind enough to read earlier versions of this book and make useful suggestions. Among them were Ian Bassin, Susan Fairbairn, Richard Rothstein, Steve Wasserman, Lawrence Weschler, my wife, Joan Andersson, my daughter, Emma Andersson, and my daughter-in-law, Lisa Hageman. If any mistakes have eluded my attention and crept into the text, they are my responsibility alone. If you spot one, please contact me so it can be corrected.

References

Since this short book is a call to action rather than a work of scholarship or journalism, I have not footnoted the facts cited. However, all the information comes from reliable sources easily available to the public. Here is the list of articles, books, reports, charts, tables, graphs and websites I used in writing the book. They document all the claims made. Given the dynamic nature of the student loan crisis and the ever-changing attempts to resolve it, new information is likely to appear with some regularity.

Bernstein, Noah S., "4 Disturbing Ways Big Banks Have Turned Colleges Into Money-Grubbing Institutions," October 3, 2012, http://www.alternet.org/4-disturbing-ways-big-banks-have-turned-colleges-money-grubbing-institutions?page=0%2C0&akid=9485.20504.mFBwRn&rd=1&src=newsletter721247&t=3&paging=off&current_page=1#bookmark

Brown, Meta and Caldwell, Sydnee, "Young Student Loan Borrowers Retreat From Housing And Auto Markets," Federal Reserve Bank of New York, April 178, 2013, http://libertystreeteconomics.newyorkfed.org/2013/04/young-student-loan-borrowers-retreat-from-housing-and-auto-markets.html

Buchheit, Paul, "Three Way the Rich and Powerful Have Cheated Young Americans," July 9, 2012, http://www.nationofchange.org/three-ways-rich-and-powerful-have-cheated-young-americans-1341846413

Burbank, John, "Pay It Forward, The Debt-Free Degree Plan for Oregon," Presentation to the Oregon Higher Education Committee, February 25, 2013.

Cersonsky, James, "5 Ways Student Debt Resistance Is Taking Off," October 25, 2013, http://www.alternet.org/education/5-ways-student-debt-resistance-taking?page=0%2C0&akid=11086.20504.LSvFj7&rd=1&src=newsletter915769&t=21

Choma, Russ, "Members of Congress Feel Student Loan Pain Firsthand," Open Secrets, February7, 2013, http://www.alternet.org/economy/members-congress-feel-student-loan-pain-firsthand?akid=10025.20504.64kuVE&rd=1&src=newsletter791205&t=19

Consumer Financial Protection Bureau, "Private Student Loans," Report to the Senate Committee on Banking, Housing, and Urban Affairs," July 20, 2012.

Democracy Now, "Matt Taibbi: We're Saddling College Students With Crushing Debt…And The Government Is Acting Like A Greedy Profiteer," August 20, 2013, http://www.alternet.org/economy/matt-taibbi-were-saddling-college-students-crushing-debt-and-govt-acting-greedy-profiteer?akid=10831.20504.MPxNfZ&rd=1&src=newsletter885243&t=3.

Durden, Tyler, "The Student Loan Bubble In 19

Simple Charts," Zero Hedge, September 28, 2012, http://www.zerohedge.com/news/2012-09-28/student-loan-bubble-19-simple-charts

Eaton, Charlie and Stewart, Brian, "Wall Street & California's Student Debt Crisis," Center on Culture, Organizations and Politics, UC Berkeley, http://d3n8a8pro7vhmx.cloudfront.net/makebankspay/pages/1/attachments/original/1383168373/Wall_Street_and_the_CA_Student_Debt_Crisis.pdf?1383168373

Economic Opportunity Institute, "Pay It Forward: Debt-Free Access To Higher Education," October 17, 2013, http://www.eoionline.org/education/higher-education/pay-it-forward-debt-free-access-to-higher-education-2/

Edelman, Peter, So Rich, So Poor: Why It's So Hard to End Poverty in America, New Press, 2012.

Edsall, Thomas Byrne, The Age of Austerity: How Scarcity Will Remake American Politics, Random House, 2012.

Ellis, Blake, "Student Debt Delays Spending, Saving – And Marriage," CNN Money, May 9, 2013.

Federal Reserve Bank of New York, "Household Debt and Credit: Student Debt," February 28, 2013, http://www.newyorkfed.org/newsevents/mediaadvisory/2013/Lee022813.pdf

Frank, Thomas, "From Ph.D to Escort: How Debt Can Change Students," Harpers, May 17, 2012.

Greene, Kelly, "New Peril for Parents: Their Kids' Student Loans," The Wall Street Journal, October 26,

2012

Grim, Ryan and Wrigley, Will, "Elizabeth Warren: Student Loans Should Have Same Rate Big Banks Get," Huffington Post, May 8, 2013.

Hacker, Andrew, "We're More Unequal Than You Think," New Review of Books, February 23, 2012.

Hacker, Jacob S. and Pierson, Paul, Winner-Take-All Politics: How Washington Made The Rich Richer – And Turned Its Back On The Middle Class, Simon & Schuster, 2010.

Institute for College Access & Success, "The Project on Student Debt," http://projectonstudentdebt.org

Jackson, Jesse, "More Youth Priced Out Of College," Chicago Sun-Times, March 18, 2013

Jamrisko, Michelle and Kolet, Ilan, "Cost of College Degree in U.S. Soars 12 Fold," August 15, 2012, Bloomberg News, http://www.bloomberg.com/news/2012-08-15/cost-of-college-degree-in-u-s-soars-12-fold-chart-of-the-day.html

Jesse, David, "Government Books $41.3 Billion In Student Loan Profits," Detroit Free Press, November 25, 2013.

Kingkade, Tyler, "Private Student Loan Study By Consumer Financial Protection Bureau Finds Parallels To Housing Market," Huffington Post, July 19, 2012.

Kingkade, Tyler, "Pell Grants Cover Smallest Portion Of College Costs In History As GOP Calls For Cuts," Huffington Post, August 29, 2012.

Kingkade, Tyler, "Student Loan Debt Ranking By State Shows Continued Rise," Huffington Post, October 18, 2012.

Kingkade, Tyler, "Elizabeth Warren's Student Loan Bill Collects More Support From College Presidents," Huffington Post, June 27, 2013.

Kingkade, Tyler, "Elizabeth Warren Calls For Big Changes To Student Loans," Huffington Post, September 29, 2013.

Lewin, Tamar, "Child's Education, but Parents' Crushing Loans," New York Times, November 11, 2012.

Lieber, Ron, "Last Plea on School Loan: Proving a Hopeless Future," New York Times, August 31, 2012.

Lieber, Ron, "Battling College Costs, a Paycheck at a Time," New York Times, February 9 2013.

Long, Katherine, "UW Tuition: What's Behind The Rising Cost?" Seattle Times, September21, 2013.

Lowrey, Annie, "Student Debt Slows Growth as Young Spend Less, New York Times, May 10, 2013.

Martin, Andrew, "Slowly, as Student Debt Rises, Colleges Confront Costs," New York Times, May 14, 2012.

Martin, Andrew, "Debt Collectors Cashing In On Student Loans," New York Times, September 8, 2012.

Martin, Andrew, "Building a Showcase Campus, Using an I.O.U.," New York Times, December 13,

2012.

Martin, Andrew and Lehren, Andrew W., "A Generation Hobbled by the Soaring Cost of College," New York Times, May 12, 2012.

Meltz, Robert, "When Congressional Legislation Interferes With Existing Contracts: Legal Issues," Congressional Research Service, August20, 2012.

Nasiripour, Shahien, "High Student Debt Poses Risk to Growth, Federal Reserve Says," Huffington Post, April 10, 2013.

Nasiripour, Shahien, "Student Loan Rate Boost Government Profit As Debt Damps Economy," Huffington Post, April 17, 2013.

Nasiripour, Shahien, "Kirsten Gillibrand Aims To Jumpstart Student Loan Refinancings With New Bill," Huffington Post, May 19, 2013.

Nasiripour, Shahien, "Federal Reserve Not Helping Student Loan Borrowers, Top Official Says," Huffington Post, June 26, 2013.

Nasiripour, Shahien, "Student Loan Deal Reached In Senate Threatens To Raise Future Costs," Huffington Post, July 11, 2013.

Nasiripour, Shahien, "Student Loan Servicing Beset By Problems Faces Calls For Overhaul," Huffington Post, October 22, 2013.

Nasiripour, Shahien, "Education Department Records Student Loan Profit For First Time Since 2000," Huffington Post, October 30, 2013.

Nasiripour, Shahien, "Education Department Books

Student Loan Profit," Huffington Post, November 18, 2013.

Nasiripour, Shahien, "Federal Student Loan Profits Help Duncan Cut Education Spending To Lowest Level Since 2001," Huffington Post, November 18, 2013.

Nasiripour, Shahien and Grim, Ryan, "Sallie Mae Profit Boosts College Endowments and Pension Funds As Students Pay More," Huffington Post, May 9, 2013.

Nasiripour, Shahien and Kirkham, "Chris, Student Loan Defaults Surge To Highest Level in Nearly 2 Decades," Huffington Post, September 30, 2013.

National Center for Education Statistics, Digest of Education Statistics, http://nces.ed.gov/programs/digest/d11/tables/dt11_008.asp

New, Catherine, "Consumer Financial Protection Bureau finds Student, Mortgage Lenders Have 'Uncanny Resemblance,'" Huffington Post, October 16, 2012.

New York Times, "Student Debt Debacles," Editorial, October 24, 2012.

New York Times, "Relief for Student Borrowers," Editorial, December 31, 2012.

Oliff, Phil et al, ""Recent Deep State Higher Education Cuts May Harm Students and the Economy For Years," Center on Budget and Policy Priorities, March 19 2013. http://www.cbpp.org/cms/index.cfm?fa=view&id=39

Packer, George, "The Broken Contract: Inequality And American Decline," Foreign Affairs, November/December, 2011.

Schwab, Klaus (ed.), "The Global Competitiveness Report, 2012-2013," World Economic Forum, http://www3.weforum.org/docs/WEF_GlobalCompetitivenessReport_2012-13.pdf

Smith, Hedrick, Who Stole The American Dream? Ransom House, 2012.

Stanford Center on Poverty and Inequality, "20 Facts About U.S. Inequality that Everyone Should Know, http://www.stanford.edu/group/scspi/cgi-bin/facts.php

State Higher Education Executive Officers Association, "State Higher Education Finance Report, 2012, http://www.sheeo.org/projects/shef-—-state-higher-education-finance

Stiglitz, Joseph, Interview on Alternet.org, June 25, 2012.

The Economist, "Student Loans in America, The Next Big Credit Bubble," October 29, 2011.

The Economist, "Students Are Drowning In Debt," April 15, 2011.

Toal, Kaye, "Hey, Recent Grads! Enjoy Burning Your Diplomas For Warmth," http://www.upworthy.com/hey-recent-grads-enjoy-burning-your-diploma-for-warmth?c=upw1

U.S. Department of Education, Office of the Inspector General, Press release, "Sallie Mae Pays $3.4 Million

To Settle Civil False Claims Act Allegations, January 5, 2001, http://www2.ed.gov/about/offices/list/oig/invtreports/ma12001.html

U.S. Department of Education, "Default Rates Rise for Federal Student Loans," September 12, 2011, http://www.ed.gov/news/press-releases/default-rates-rise-federal-student-loans

Wang, Marian, "Banks' Lending Frenzy Left Borrowers Buried In Student Debt," ProPublica.org, July 20, 2012.

Wang, Marian, "Obamacare Is Complicating Some Student Loans," Propublica, April 23, 2012.